ON THE EDGE

HOW MY **CRAPPY** JOB CHANGED MY **LIFE**

ON THE EDGE

HOW MY **CRAPPY** JOB CHANGED MY **LIFE**

STUART EDGE

Plain Sight Publishing
An Imprint of Cedar Fort, Inc.
Springville, Utah

ISBN 13: 978-1-4621-1854-0

Published by Plain Sight Publishing, an imprint of Cedar Fort, Inc.
2373 W. 700 S., Springville, UT 84663
Distributed by Cedar Fort, Inc., www.cedarfort.com

LIBRARY OF CONGRESS CATALOGING-IN-PUBLICATION DATA

Names: Edgington, Stuart, 1989- author. | Heirtzler, Robyn, author.
Title: On the edge / Stuart Edgington with Robyn Heirtzler.
Description: Springville, Utah : Plain Sight Publishing, an imprint of Cedar
Fort, Inc., [2016] | Includes bibliographical references and index.
Identifiers: LCCN 2016003415 (print) | LCCN 2016005790 (ebook) | ISBN
9781462118540 (perfect bound : alk. paper) | ISBN 9781462126460 (epub,
pdf, mobi)
Subjects: LCSH: Edgington, Stuart, 1989- | Self-actualization (Psychology) |
Self-help techniques.
Classification: LCC BF637.S4 E387 2016 (print) | LCC BF637.S4 (ebook) | DDC
158--dc23
LC record available at http://lccn.loc.gov/2016003415

Cover design by Krystal Wares and Kinsey Beckett
Cover design © 2016 Cedar Fort, Inc.
Edited and typeset by Rebecca Bird

Printed in the United States of America

10 9 8 7 6 5 4 3 2 1

Printed on acid-free paper

CONTENTS

CONTENTS

PREFACE

What's up, guys? Stuart Edge here with my new book, *On the Edge*, your full-blown Edgeucation of all things Stuart Edge!

To be completely open with you, I've gotten personal in this book about my childhood, the anxiety I experienced during my early teenage years, and my move to Mexico shortly thereafter. I've been up-front about my religious beliefs and how my morals have played a huge part in my journey from porta-potty cleaner (yes, I really used to clean porta-potties . . . I didn't just do it for a cool book cover) to "social influencer" or as you may prefer to call me, a "YouTuber."

I've shared some of my secrets of success, dating horror stories, and a few of my hopes and dreams (at least the ones I'm aware of). One thing I didn't share was all the secrets to my magic tricks. I'm pretty sure you can find those online anyway.

Even though the subtitle of this book is *How My Crappy Job Changed My Life*, it wasn't just one job that influenced me. While it's literal in a sense, it's more of a figurative message that shows how hard times, or "crappy moments," have given me the experience I need to overcome life's challenges and succeed in my career. I hope as you read this book you will begin to see how *your* crappy job, or experiences, can change *your* life.

ACKNOWLEDGMENTS

Wow, I cannot believe this book is actually done now! When I started writing, I had no idea how much time and energy it would take. There were many writing sessions that started in the early evening and ended the next afternoon. If anyone out there is considering writing a book, do it. I learned so much about myself and it was a good reminder that I have done hard things in the past and I am capable of doing so much more.

This book would not have been possible without the sacrifices of so many friends and family members.

Mom, thank you for encouraging me to keep working on this book, even when I wanted to give up so many times. Also, thank you for being willing to take the two-hour drive from Logan to Provo at one in the morning, just to help me finish it.

Aunt Diane, thank you as well for the late nights you put into this book, and for sacrificing so much of your time and talents to make sure I was confident in what I was doing.

Kelly Wilkins and Maille Coombs, "you da real MVPs." I will never be able to repay you for how much time you willingly gave me over the last few weeks of writing this book. I am forever grateful for your friendship. Thank you for your patience with me!

ACKNOWLEDGMENTS

Robyn Heirtzler, thank you for putting so much of your energy and soul into helping write this book. I would have never known where to start or what thoughts to put on the pages had it not been for the countless hours you spent reading my journals and letting me yap your ear off so you could know which stories were most important in my life and which ones to include in the book. You are the best. I hope you continue to have lots of success in life.

Also thank you to the team at Cedar Fort, Inc. for giving me the chance to write this book and for their hard work and patience with me throughout the process!

Outside of writing the book, there are countless others that have been there for me.

Dad, thanks for your example to me. You teach me so much through your actions alone. I am proud you call you my dad.

Stephen and Spencer, thank you for being the world's best brothers. I love how much fun we can have together. My favorite video I've ever done is still the "Egg Roulette Challenge" you helped me with. You both did so much for me when we lived together last year. It changed me completely.

Caleb Hunter, you were seriously the best mission companion and then college roommate anyone could ask for. Your example to me the first few months of my mission was crucial to my success during the rest of the mission and your advice after that played a huge part in my success in my career. Te amo, amigo.

To all the other roommates I have had, Winston Behle, Jason Rane, Nate Turley, Nate Smeding, Blake Hill, Preston Merchant, James Thompson, Ben Cheng, Keith Allen, and Nate Bonham, your friendships and examples to me are priceless. Also, thank you soooo much for your patience. I know I am not the easiest person to live with. I'm sure many of you have been woken up by me in the middle of the night wanting

ACKNOWLEDGMENTS

to get your opinion on a video I was editing or to tell you about a new idea I had just come up with and if you thought it would be a viral video. The fact you were just there and listened has done so much for me.

Tyler Stevens, I can't tell you how grateful I am for you offering to get me a job at Orabrush. You forever changed my life. Thank you for being in the right place at the right time.

Kaitlin Snow, thank you for teaching me how to edit! You are the best editor I know and was honored to be able to look over your shoulder for six months and learn from the best.

Austin Craig, your belief in me from the moment you met me has gotten me through many tough times. Thank you.

And to the Harmon brothers, Jeff, Daniel, and Neal, thank you for having faith in me and helping me get to where I am now.

RJ Idos, Wex Lee, Andrew Hales, Marcus Joseph, Peter Hollens, Kevin Herrera, Jesse Wride, Shane Rickard, AP Guerrero, Jarek 1:20, Britney Lavatai, Melanie Myler . . . your help with making my videos and your friendship has meant the world to me and I hope someday I can repay you for all the good you have done in my life.

And the people I would like to give the most thanks to are you. There are so many of you out there that have been reading this book and that have been watching me from the moment I started making videos. I feel so indebted to you and know that I wouldn't be where I am today if it weren't for your support. Thank you for always being there for me.

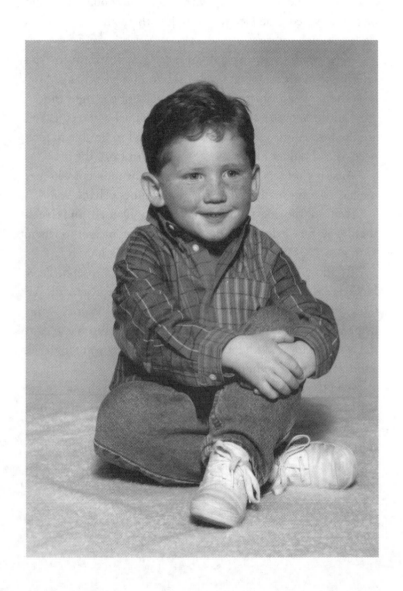

INTRODUCTION

I almost didn't write this book and it was for one big reason:

I'm not done yet.

Early in 2014, I got an email from a publishing company suggesting I write a book about my life story. I'd seen a few of my friends' books, and it looked like they were having a lot of success, but even still, I felt conflicted. I didn't want the fact that I was writing a book to make it seem like I'm content with where I am at this moment in my life. But then again, I have had some amazing stories that could help people reach for their own dreams and achieve them. Knowing I could inspire, but knowing I wasn't "done" was driving me crazy and making the decision much harder.

As I thought about it some more, I came to the conclusion that no one is ever really "done." At least, I know *I'm* not done. Yes, for the past few years, I've had lots of success making videos online, but I'm not convinced I'll be performing magic tricks on YouTube for the rest of my life. (Not that there's anything wrong with making magic trick videos . . . I've just got some other interests I'd like to pursue as well.)

I'll be honest—it's scary thinking this way, because it means in order for me to feel like I'm progressing in life, I need to leave my successes and comfort zones, and venture off into unfamiliar territory with the chance of failure or heartbreak in the process. (Raise your hand if you like having your heart broken. No one? Okay. Let's continue.)

When I think about my life and my future, I feel the best chapters have yet to be written. Who knows? I may get married one day and have all these little babies running around, threatening to push me over the edge. I could end up touring the world as a famous musician or becoming the host of my own talk show. Maybe I'll even become the president of the United States! (Though I really hope that isn't in my destiny because, to me, that doesn't sound fun.) It seems as though there is an endless list of plot lines my life could follow. My outlook on life, or my vision, could change just from the time I write this book to the time you actually read it. So just imagine what could happen in another year or two. My transformation from porta-potty cleaner to having millions of views on my YouTube channel happened almost overnight—so changes happen, and they can happen pretty fast.

Rest assured, this isn't a book full of blank pages. I obviously decided to go ahead with writing the book and, even though I feel the best chapters of my life *are* still blank, there are lots of pages in my book of life that are filled with insights and experiences that could benefit a few people out there.

As you read this, be prepared. I've separated my life into three parts:

PART 1: THE FORMATIVE YEARS 1989–2010

Before I get into how I started making YouTube videos, it's important I explain my childhood. The experiences I had in elementary school, the anxiety I dealt with during middle school, and the self-discovery I had throughout high school leading up to and including missionary service for my church all had major impacts on my character and personality. The reasons I think the way I do and make the decisions I do are in large part due to the experiences I had when I was younger. I feel there are more hidden gems about how to be successful at your craft in these chapters than any of the others.

PART 2: IT ALL STARTS TO COME TOGETHER
2010–2012

Once returning home from my two years of service as a full-time missionary, I remember thinking *Oh wow . . . life is starting now.* These chapters explain my life as a young single adult trying to figure out what I wanted to do for a career, while balancing work, school, and yes, even dating. They cover my experience working at an elementary school and later how I fell into the porta-potty business and how that set the stage for a life-changing realization.

PART 3: VIRAL VIDEOS
2012–PRESENT

The exciting part about these chapters is that this is where *you* come into the story. Yep, you! From this point on in the book, it's where many of you were introduced to my life. While you may not have known me personally, you saw the videos that I talk about here. This is kind of like the "Behind the Scenes of Stuart Edge" part of the book. I talk about what was going on in my mind during my rise in YouTube fame and I explain the pains and struggles of being a YouTuber and having so many people watching me. I get very personal about the feelings I felt during my most down moments. I also leave you with some lasting words of wisdom and a final "testimony," if you will.

INTRODUCTION

There's one last thing I wanted to mention in this introduction:

Sticky notes.

To me, ideas are priceless. Even before ideas became moneymakers, I treasured them. I remember getting most of my ideas at night though, and if I waited until morning to write them down I'd forget them. I actually started sleeping with a pad of sticky notes next to me so I could write on them as soon as an idea formed in my head. Some mornings I'd wake up to find sticky notes all over the wall.

> *IDEAS ARE A DIME A DOZEN. THE ABILITY TO EXECUTE THOSE IDEAS IS PRICELESS.*

Eventually I started using a whiteboard, but seriously, sticky notes will never go out of style. It only makes sense that I'd put sticky notes of wisdom in my book.

Enjoy the read, send me a message, or comment on one of my videos if I miss anything. If I'm lucky, it'll leave you on the Edge of your seat, wondering what happens next. But don't worry; as my story progresses, and the blank chapters of my life are being filled with stories and experiences, I'll be in touch.

PART 1

THE FORMATIVE YEARS

1

A NORMAL, NOT-SO-NORMAL CHILDHOOD

If my childhood were a video game, on a difficulty scale from "Easy" to "Unbeatable," the setting would probably have been on "Normal, with Some Not-So-Normal Things Popping up Every Once in a While."

"But, Stuart, that doesn't make any sense. . . ."

I know. You're right. It doesn't really make sense. But that's exactly what it was. My childhood had a couple moments that very few kids experience, but besides that, I felt like my life was as "normal" as they come. My neighborhoods were always safe, our family never had to deal with any major illnesses or unexpected deaths, and, generally speaking, we were pretty happy. While we weren't monetary wealthy, we always had the basic necessities and were able to do fun things together.

I will say this about me though . . . as a child (and even still to this day) I was very observant. More observant than most kids my age. I loved to watch people and analyze why they did what they did. Why they interacted with others the way they did. What made them laugh, smile, and cry. When I went to movies or concerts, I paid more attention to the audience and their reactions to the performance than the performance itself. The power one person could have on the emotions of hundreds, or even thousands of people, fascinated me. However, the side effect of knowing more about other people than I knew about myself at such a young age was that I was pretty quiet for most of my childhood—people usually assumed that I was shy. Unbeknownst to me, however, it was my constant observations that were laying the foundations I would need in my life to be a great entertainer and performer.

BORN TO ENTERTAIN

Because I was constantly observing and determining what entertained people, I had this innate desire to perform and impress anyone I met. Whether it was with music, sports, or school, I always loved the idea of being in front of people, showing off what I had been working on. I definitely wasn't a child prodigy by any means, but there was always this feeling inside me that pushed me to be perform. In elementary school, I never turned down an opportunity to answer a question and my favorite day of the year was when the high school's show choir would come sing and dance for the entire school.

And while most young boys thought it was "girly" to play the violin, I joined the school orchestra because that meant three or four times a year I would get to be on that same stage in front of the whole school showing off my stuff. I guess I just wanted as many eyes on me as possible.

As confident as I was in my mind, sometimes, I wasn't always the most confident when it came time for the actual performance. I remember one time in second grade, I had signed up to give a piano performance for my entire music class. A few minutes before I was supposed to perform, my nerves got the best of me and I ran outside. My dad, who showed up to watch me, followed me out and stood with me as I cried and told him I didn't want to play in front of anyone. Just then, a girl in my class that I had a huge crush on came outside to see how I was doing. Almost immediately, I perked up and, acting all suave, told her I was just getting ready to go inside and play my song.

I think my dad remembered that moment, because a few years later in the fourth grade, when I was too nervous to present my science fair project, he told me he'd just so happened to see that same girl in the audience and, in almost the exact same fashion, I perked up, went inside, and, with that same suave attitude, presented my science fair project. To this day, I don't think anyone has given a more compelling presentation on what's inside of a golf ball.

It's easy to look at these stories and think that all my life I've just been hungry for attention. But it's much more than that. I believe I was learning to identify with what made me who I am and in what situations I felt most comfortable. Performing and entertaining were really the only times I felt like I was in my true element.

> *I BELIEVE GOD GIVES US UNIQUE TALENTS AND ABILITIES THAT MAKE UP OUR PERSONALITY. TAKE TIME TO REALLY CONNECT WITH WHAT THOSE ARE FOR YOU.*

NO REDHEADS ON TV

Even though I had this constant desire to entertain, as I looked around at my life, I felt I'd gone as far as I could because I couldn't see how it would ever be possible for me to do anything more than little piano recitals or science fairs. I remember watching the Disney Channel and talk shows and thinking how fun it would be to be in a show like that, but then looking in the mirror and thinking there probably wasn't a spot on those shows for a goofy looking, redheaded, freckle-faced kid from Utah. I wanted to be on stage, entertaining people and making them laugh, but, as far as I knew, I was the only one in the history of my family or friends who wanted anything like that. As far as my parents went, my mom was a teacher and my dad engineered treadmills. As a kid I thought, *How could they give advice on becoming a movie star, when they have no experience in that field?*

THE PERFORMANCE THAT CHANGED ME

There was one performance that had a lasting impact on me.

When I was in the fifth grade, I really wanted to participate in the school talent show. Ever since I'd done a book report on Harry Houdini back in the second grade, I had an interest in magic. I ordered a small magic book from a catalog I'd found at my school and figured I'd teach myself a few tricks to prepare for the tryout. I had no idea how much deciding to learn magic for that talent show would affect me as a future entertainer

You see, most of my performances up to this point had been as part of a group or team, or expressing my voice through an instrument. This was one of the first times where *I* would be in the spotlight. There was no tension or pressure to be like anyone else, just freedom to be whoever I wanted to be.

The tryout day came and, unfortunately, I hadn't mastered my main trick yet, so I just gave a really good explanation of what I thought it would look like. Somehow I made it through and was scheduled as one of the closing acts for the show. The day of the show finally arrived and as I stepped onto that familiar elementary school stage for the first time as a solo performer, I felt like that was where I belonged.

My nerves were calm, my palms dry and steady on the deck of cards as I shuffled them. The words I'd rehearsed flowed easily and before I knew it, I was telling jokes and actually hearing laughter in response.

"You know what I call magic?" I asked. I paused to build some tension for the punch line, then said, "Putting a coin in a soda machine and having it magically turn it into a drink."

Only about half of them laughed at my joke, but regardless, I was having fun.

I continued with the performance and called to the stage my friend Tanner, who I had previously instructed what he should do when he was called up. As he walked onto the stage, I asked him to select any card from the deck in my hands and put it inside the envelope I had placed on the table in front of us.

"Because I am a magician," I told him, "I will be able to magically make it so the card you put in the envelope is a completely different card." I could sense the audience's anticipation to see how and *if* it was even possible. Tanner followed the instructions I gave him and then, after I said a few magic words, I opened the envelope only to discover that it was the same card. *Wait, what? How was that possible? It was supposed to be a completely different card!* I quickly thought about what could have gone wrong. Then I realized Tanner must have forgotten to flip the envelope over, like I instructed him to before the show. Doing so would have dropped down the secret flap in the envelope, which would place a new card on top, covering the old one. In that moment when I could have panicked, got embarrassed, and ran off stage, for some reason my little fifth

SOMETIMES THINGS JUST DON'T WORK. . . . AND THAT'S LIFE.

grade self was so calm. I simply told the audience it didn't work and went on to another trick.

I messed up on the card trick, but it didn't matter. I honestly don't remember what happened after that or how my act ended. The feeling I had when I stood in front of my entire school, and had all the students laughing at my jokes, was all I needed to remember.

As I returned home at the end of the day, I was filled with confidence. Yeah, there were still ups and downs at home, but I was finally learning more about myself and doing the things that brought me joy.

2

BE PREPARED

When I wasn't busy finding ways to get on a stage in front of a few hundred of my peers, you would most likely find me having fun outside. One of my favorite things to do was camping. I loved leaving the warmth of the valley and traveling up into the mountains where the air grew thinner and the night became colder. As much as I loved camping with my friends and family, I mostly looked forward to when I would turn twelve and get to go on my first ever campout as a Boy Scout.

My twelfth birthday came and I officially joined the Boy Scouts of America. Shortly after, our troop began planning our summer campout. It was a little less than a year after the elementary school talent show and the energy and confidence I felt that day on stage seemed to carry itself over to all other areas of my life. I could hardly wait for the campout. Little did I know, however, that the Scout camp experience that was awaiting me would have a major impact on my life. The Scout motto is "Be Prepared," but there was no way I could prepare for what was about to happen.

AN EMOTIONAL WAR ZONE

I'd heard all about how fun the Scout campouts were from some of the older boys in my troop—the swimming, the canoeing, the campfire stories, and the cute nurse's aides that worked at the lodge. I was so excited for everything they talked about, except for maybe the nurses—I thought I was too young to care about that.

For the first few days, I enjoyed myself. It was so fun! While I did miss my family a little, I liked being away from home with a group of my friends, running around and setting things on fire (mainly just marshmallows). I had no idea, however, there was an emotional bomb waiting to be dropped on my entire Scout camp experience. I'm sure if it was an actual physical bomb, it would have been labeled "Homesickness" and the name would have been spray painted in thick black, unfriendly looking letters, with a scary face on the nose of it.

Bombs away! happened on day three when a care package was sent up to the campground we were staying at. I remember I was in my tent and everyone started calling my name. I crawled outside to see a small group of my friends and camp leaders circled around a big brown cardboard box on a table with my name on it.

"Looks like someone sent you a package!" one of the leaders explained. We opened it up to find it packed full of chocolate milk and chocolate chip cookies . . . two of my favorite snacks from home. Word got out that it was for everyone to share so, like wolves on a fresh piece of meat, a pack of sugar-hungry teenage boys began to rip the box apart. Sometime during that commotion, someone handed me a note with my name on it that was in the box. I opened it and began to read it to myself.

Dear Stuart,

I hope you are having a wonderful Scout camp experience! I miss you a lot, and am so blessed to have you as a son. I can't wait for you to come home.

Love, Mom

That note, although very kind and sweet, was not the thing a preteen boy needed to read while up camping with his friends. I could feel the "Homesickness" bomb crashing into the ground, setting off a fiery wave of explosion that shattered my emotions like a fragile glass building. I began to realize how much I missed my mom and my family and that I really wanted to go home. I had never felt anything like this before. What happened to the months of unshaken confidence I'd had after my magic show and leading up to this campout? I sat in my tent, crying for almost an hour. At least I could pretend that tent was my home for now. But to make matters worse, later that afternoon I had to leave the safe haven of my tent to spend an entire night freezing under a stupid lean-to for my Wilderness Survival merit badge.

SURVIVAL OF THE FITTEST

We were supposed to pair off with a buddy, hike thirty minutes away from our camp, and build a shelter out of sticks and leaves that could protect us through the night. I was so distracted by my emotions that I didn't have time to help my friend set up a good shelter for us. We were running out of daylight, so we asked two of the older boys if we could stay in their shelter, but it was obvious that we wouldn't all fit. Since it was nearly dark, the only option we had was to put our sleeping bags between the two thin blue tarps we were allowed to bring with us, and try to find shelter in there.

As I crawled into my tarp to try to get some rest and forget the day, a group of Scouts walked past pointing out that we

> DURING TIMES OF HIGH STRESS, SOMETIMES THE ONLY RELIEF COMES BY GETTING SOME REST AND STARTING OVER AGAIN IN THE MORNING.

had made our camp right next to a badger hole! If my emotions weren't going to kill me in the night, then an old angry badger definitely would. I said my prayers and then covered myself up as much as I could hoping the flimsy tarp would somehow protect me from the dangerously sharp claws of our new neighbor while I slept. I stared into the night sky, grateful at least I had a friend next to me and that we had some form of shelter . . . even if it was just a couple of tarps. To me they felt like solid concrete walls, sheltering me from all the craziness that happened that day.

PUTTING THE "SICK" IN "HOMESICK"

Somehow, I survived that night and woke up in one piece. As I walked back to the main campsite the next morning, I couldn't stop thinking about home. Upon arriving back at camp, I snuck away to the lodge so I could call my mom from the pay phone they had outside. "Come get me now!" I cried through the phone as soon as I heard her voice. I could sense that my mom wasn't sure what to do. I think we both knew this was an opportunity for me to learn and grow, but I didn't want anything to do with camping anymore. After a few minutes of chatting on the phone, my mom suggested I stay out the rest of the week and just call her anytime I felt nervous again.

I wish I could say I hung up the phone and skipped back to camp whistling the tune to a camp song and talking to all the little forest creatures, but that's not even close to what happened. I started my way back to our group campsite and, for a moment, I thought I was going to be fine, but gradually, my emotional homesick feeling turned into actual physical sickness. I felt dizzy and my stomach hurt. I was a mess. I tried to go to the merit badge classes, thinking it would help get my mind off home, but I just kept feeling even sicker. The next day it got so bad, I ended up telling one of our group leaders how sick I felt, and he took me to the nurse's station in the lodge. While I was in there, I could still hear other campers running around and having fun outside. "Don't you guys miss your families?" I thought. "How could you be so insensitive and selfish, and not be bawling your eyes out on the floor because you are away from the people that love you the most!? Why are you not miserable like me right now!?"

We told the nurse my symptoms and she suggested I was probably just homesick, and I could stay in the little hospital bed and rest until I felt ready to return back to the normal scouting activities. Almost immediately, a sense of relief came

HOW MANY TIMES IN LIFE DO WE THINK THAT IF WE AREN'T PUSHING OURSELVES TO THE MAX, WE AREN'T BEING SUCCESSFUL?

MY ADVICE TO YOU IS IN THOSE CRAPPY MOMENTS, DON'T THINK YOU'RE WEAK OR A FAILURE IF YOU NEED SOME TIME TO REST AND REJUVENATE. NO ONE CAN GIVE IT THEIR ALL, ALL OF THE TIME.

over me. I lay on that little bed deep in thought, amazed that I was starting to feel better. I may not have fully comprehended it then, but as I look back now, I realize, all I needed was to give myself a small break from the things that were bringing me stress at the time. I wasn't quitting; I was taking a break.

I think my body loved the comfort of sleeping in a real bed again far away from anything that was higher on the food chain than me, because I ended up falling asleep in the infirmary bed and slept there all through the night. In the morning, I was awakened by what I thought were two angels. *Did I die last night?* I remember thinking. Turns out it was just the nurse's aides. I guess the stories were true.

BACK TO "NORMAL"

I ended up feeling better enough to rejoin with my scout group for the final evening of camp. We had a closing testimony meeting and a great dinner and we laughed at all the fun things that happened while we were there. That last night around the campfire, I was so impressed that no one in my troop made fun of me for being homesick (maybe they were just jealous I got to hang out with the nurses). I went to bed that night feeling like I just had the best scout camp experience of my life, regardless of what may have happened. The next morning we packed up our things and headed back to our families.

It wasn't long before I was back to doing the things I loved. What happened at Scout camp was a thing of the past, and I was now looking forward to my next adventure as a growing adolescent. I felt happy, but what I couldn't see was how the anxiety from homesickness left me emotionally vulnerable; one more anxiety-filled moment might make me snap.

3

STRETCHED PAST
THE BREAKING POINT

About a month after Scout camp, and toward the start of the seventh grade, I asked my mom to sign me up to play American Football. Growing up, I loved playing sports . . . I guess I've always loved the feeling of competition. I tried nearly every sport and was pretty good at most of them. Well, except soccer. At the young age of five, I learned that fútbol was not the sport for me. Let me explain . . .

We were only a few games into the season and the coach decided to give me the important job of protecting the goal. I threw on the oversized goalie shirt and stood in the goalie box for the first time in my (short) soccer career. As I watched the other players try to score on the other end of the field, my eye caught hold of a butterfly that landed on a dandelion a few feet in front of me. Its fluttering wings seemed to call my name. I walked up to the dandelion it was resting on and plucked it right out of the ground. As you'd expect, the butterfly was startled and started flying away. As I watched it fly off, I heard people cheering my name. I looked toward the sideline at the cheering crowd and noticed they were all pointing at something. I seriously wondered if they were cheering that I found a cool butterfly. For some reason they kept looking at me, yelling, and pointing. *These people are weird*, I thought.

It's just a butterfly. Their pointing became more aggressive, so I looked up field in the direction they were signaling. I'm not sure when, but at some point during my butterfly expedition, I must have wanted to get closer to the ground because I was now sitting in the grass, plucking dandelions as the opposing team charged toward me with the ball. I tried to make some sort of defensive move as quickly as I could, but it was too late. The ball hit the back of the net and the opposing team scored.

I figured the only way to redeem myself from such an embarrassing moment was to join a sport where if I ever dozed off again, I had the potential to be knocked clean off my feet . . . so that's why I picked American football.

IF SOMEONE KNOCKS YOU DOWN, GET BACK UP

Practice was held on some fields near the local high school about four miles from my house. Most of the time I would get a ride to and from practice with a friend on the team who lived in the same area. But that day, my mom was able to drop me off.

Practice that day started off kind of like the typical practice. The coach had us do some warm-up runs and then a few technique drills. I cringed, however, when he called out for us to get in position for a blocking drill. Basically everyone got in a big circle and two people laid down on their backs in the middle. When the coach blew his whistle, both players would roll over as quickly as they could, stand up, and try to hit the other person out of the circle. The faster person would have the advantage because they would hit first. I hated this drill because I was the smallest kid on the team, and my pads were too big for me, making it hard to be agile.

He told us to partner off, and then he started running the drill. The kid who I usually partnered off with, who was big, but slow, wasn't there that day, so I had to partner off with

CHAPTER 3

a different kid. His name was Tyson and he was strong and quick. Anyone could jump in at anytime, so usually, my regular partner and I would jump in early, and then kind of sneak to the back of the circle and wait for the drill to be over. My partner today though seemed to want to jump in every time. Right off the bat, he jumped in the circle. I was forced to enter as well. I laid on my back, hoping maybe for some reason the coach would decide to do a different drill, even though we just got started. My heart was racing and I was praying that I would not look like a fool. The sound of the whistle rang through the air and I began the struggle of fighting against my oversized shoulder pads to roll over and stand up. I rolled over as quickly as I could, feeling like it was the fastest I had ever done. *Maybe I might be first to hit*, I thought. *That would feel so great if I hit first.* I was standing up in position when *bam*, a huge strong body pushed up against my helmet and chest, knocking my feet into the air and sending me right on the ground. *Ouch.* I knew it must have looked worse than it felt because everyone let out an "oooh." I got up, shook myself off, and walked back to the outside of the circle.

Well, at least I did my turn, and now I could just wait it out—what? Again? It must have been no more than a minute, and my partner was jumping back into the circle. *Oh my, this kid is going to get me killed*, I thought. I lay down and waited for the whistle. I did not want this to turn into a life-or-death situation, so I anticipated when the coach might blow the whistle. I guessed right, because as soon as I heard it blow, I felt I was already halfway rolled over. *I'm going to do it this time*, I thought. I quickly stood up and *bam!* Same thing. I was picked up off my feet and driven straight into the ground. This was the most embarrassing practice I'd ever had.

I tried to hide in the back of the circle but every minute or so my partner would jump back into the circle, and every time, it would be the same result. Once I got up at the same time as him, but I was so beat from all the other times, that he just pushed me back with ease and drove me into the ground.

LEFT ALONE

It seemed like that was the only thing we did that day, because shortly after the drill was over, our coach told us we could all go home. I picked up my gear and left as quickly as I could, just in case the coach changed his mind and decided to run that drill again. I ran to the corner where my mom usually picked me up and threw my sore body onto the ground. I couldn't wait to get home, take a shower, and forget all about practice.

NOTE TO FUTURE SELF: IF YOU EVER HAVE KIDS THAT PLAY FOOTBALL, MAKE SURE THEIR EQUIPMENT IS THE RIGHT SIZE. IT WILL SAVE THEM A WHOLE LOT OF TROUBLE.

About ten minutes had passed and there was still no sign of my mom. Maybe she was just held up by something, and she would be there in a few minutes. I watched as, one by one, my fellow teammates' parents came, picked them up, and left. Pretty soon there wasn't a single player left on the field. I started to get nervous. Did something bad happen to my family? Were they safe?

It was dark now and I decided I'd need to find my own way home. I saw the football field lights were on at the high school, so I figured I'd start there. There was a powder puff game going on and I hoped I'd see someone I knew, but as I scanned the faces in the bleachers, all I saw were strangers. The older boys shouted to the players; the girls laughed and threw their shoulders back, pretending to be as tough as their opponents. I didn't care about either team. I just wanted to go home.

I turned back to the practice field, dragging my feet through the brittle grass, my helmet banging my shins as my shoulders slumped forward. I had no money for a pay phone and cell phones didn't exist back then. Home was too far away to walk—about an hour and a half—so I just sat there, trying to think of another plan.

At this point people were starting to leave the powder puff game. If someone there couldn't take me home, then there was surely no one else in the area that could be of service. I started to panic. What was going to happen to me? Would my family notice I was gone? Were they even alive? What if they thought I was already home and in bed? Would this practice field be my bed tonight? What if I was kidnapped? The feeling of anxiety was setting in. I was feeling suffocated by the fear inside of me. Somehow, in all the commotion, I began to pray out loud. "God, what is happening to me? Help me, help me. Please. Pleeeease!"

Cars whizzed by, concerned parents picking their children up from the game. I tried to block it out until one car rolled to a stop a few feet away.

"Are you okay?" A woman's voice I didn't recognize called out. I looked up. She must have seen the tears streaming down my face because her forehead creased as she leaned further toward me and asked, "Do you need a ride home?"

I nodded my head vigorously and ran up to the car. I explained my situation and told her where I lived. Besides telling her which turns to take, we didn't talk much. I didn't really have the energy to carry on a conversation. I was still too busy thinking about what might have happened.

When I walked in the front door I found out that my mom had gone to a Scout activity with one of my two younger brothers, forgetting all about me for what had felt like hours. I called the church where they were meeting, the pain raw in my throat as I asked, "How could you forget about me?" She explained that she was so sorry. She got caught up in the event she was at and honestly just forgot.

ANXIETY AT SCHOOL

Because I was still so vulnerable from the anxiety of Scout camp, something inside me snapped. This traumatic experience caused me to have symptoms similar to separation anxiety. For the next year and a half of my life I would get sudden anxiety attacks as if I was abandoned whenever I was away from my parents. Thankfully my mom was a teacher at the same school I attended, so I could swing by her classroom any time I had an anxiety attack. The attacks got worse though when she wasn't going to be there. Because of safety reasons, teachers wouldn't let a student just leave the classroom without a hall pass signed and dated by a teacher. We made a deal with the school therapist, that anytime my mom would be gone from school, I could go to her office and she would write me a hall pass. This helped a little. But my anxiety kept getting worse and sometimes, even when my mom was at school, I just needed to walk by her classroom to make sure she was there. I needed some sort of all-access hall pass that let me leave from anywhere at anytime.

One time, I swung by the therapist's office to get my hall pass because my mom would be gone that day. I waited in her office for about fifteen minutes. Anxiety creeping upon me, I really just needed my hall pass to make it through the day. A few minutes later she hurried in, said hi to me, and I explained I was there to get a hall pass. She quickly grabbed one of the hall passes from the pad in her drawer, filled in the date and time, signed it, and I was on my way.

As I looked down at the hall pass later, I noticed she filled it out in pencil! My mind began racing, I had access to an unlimited, all access hall pass, exactly what I had been waiting for! I safeguarded that hall pass with all the care in the world. Every day, before I went to school, I would erase the date on it, and update it with the current day. One day I could sense the anxiety setting in as my heart began to race and my crazy thoughts started to take control of my mind and body. Looking for a way to escape, I knew all I needed was to step outside for a moment, and I would be fine. I frantically took out the hall pass, walked up to my teacher, and showed her the crumpled white piece of paper. Would she notice the layers of dates that had been written and erased over and over again? Would she accuse me of lying, rip up my ticket out, and angrily tell me to sit back down? Without any hesitations, she took a look, and simply told me I was fine to go. I felt so free. Liberated. I walked the halls down to my mom's classroom. I reluctantly peeked in to find she was still there teaching. My pounding heart settled as a sense of relief came over me. The sight of her was enough to kill my anxiety for a small moment.

THE MAGIC HALL PASS

> DON'T FEEL THAT YOU ARE "WEAK" IF YOU SEEK PROFESSIONAL HELP FOR THE PROBLEMS YOU MAY BE FACING.

Anytime I felt an anxiety attack coming on, I would pull it out, show my teacher, and be free to roam the halls. I'd still get regular hall passes from the therapist when my mom was gone, but I never told her about the one I used on all the other days when she didn't give me one.

That little hall pass did more for me than I could have ever imagined. It was like my little magic feather. In the Disney movie *Dumbo*, Dumbo's mother dies and he is forced to perform as a clown elephant. A circus mouse points out that if Dumbo spread his giant elephant ears, he would be able to fly and would become a big star. Dumbo is too nervous to try, so the mouse gives him a feather that he says will give him the power to fly. Dumbo tries it and, sure enough, he begins to fly!

One day, while soaring high above the circus crowd in an amazing performance, Dumbo loses grip of his feather and it blows away out of reach. Dumbo panics and starts falling straight toward the ground. The circus mouse, who was accompanying Dumbo in his flight, desperately starts yelling at Dumbo, telling him the feather was a hoax and that he had the power inside him to fly the whole time. At the last moment, Dumbo listens to the mouse and opens his giant ears, soaring again above the crowd. Sorry for the spoiler alert if you've never seen *Dumbo*.[1]

Eventually, I was able to stop using my "Magic Hall Pass" and just use the passes the school counselor gave me at my request. The anxiety didn't stop; I just started to see I had the power in me to overcome those feelings. Developing that strength was crucial for me to be able to handle the problems that were about to go on at home.

DEALING WITH DIVORCE

Toward the end of my seventh grade year, my mother called me into her room one day and said, "Your father and I are separating."

I cried a little and voiced my opinion that they shouldn't do it, but I knew her mind was set.

"We just need some time," she continued.

Over the next few weeks we did a constant back and forth from spending time with my mom and my dad. That's what was sad, seeing everything I'd known my entire life change that fast. It was sad to see my dad move into a little apartment without us and know how hard it must be on him to wake up completely alone every day. I remember thinking I wish there was a "hall pass for life" I could give him, so he could just take a break from his troubles and worries. But there was no such thing, and all *my* energy was spent on trying to make it through my *own* life and not have another anxiety attack.

A couple more months went by before my mother announced that she and my father were getting divorced. I was sad. I thought of my mom raising us three boys and my dad starting over in his own little place. Of course, we'd still see him and be in his life, but it would be different without my parents being married.

THERE'S ALWAYS HOPE

Before I end this chapter, I just want to say how grateful I am for my parents. I am here today because of them. I hope what I say in the next few paragraphs will touch someone out there who may be going through a similar situation.

Divorce is a strange thing because when we talk about it, we often look for *who* to label as the "bad guy." *Who* messed up? *Who* was the one dragging everyone down? I don't blame either of my parents for getting a divorce or think one is better than the other because of it. While every case is different, if divorce is present in someone's life, I don't think it means they necessarily failed or didn't do a good job at something. I believe God has given us the wonderful gift to be able to make our own choices. No matter where we are in life because of our decisions or because of the decisions of others, if we continually turn to God, someday we will receive all the blessings He has in store for us.

MY PARENTS ARE AWESOME

Growing up, I felt like my parents were *both* such amazing people and each had more strengths than weaknesses. My dad was and still is a great example of selfless service. Countless times in my childhood after working hard to shovel the snow off our sidewalks or mow our lawn (which took almost two full hours from start to finish), I would see my dad walk over to the neighbor's house whose lawn was starting to look like a rainforest, or whose driveway was covered in feet of snow, and begin working away . . . again. He would always show up to my football or baseball games and stay there the whole time. He is still involved in my life, showing up to support me in shows or presentations. His example has made me the hardworking, caring man that I am today.

My mother was and still is such a sweet caring person. I'm always amazed at how cool she is. Maybe it's because she has taught young teenagers all her life that she stays on top of the latest trends. She always did her best to make sure our family was saying our prayers and going to church. Having to decide what she felt was the best thing for her and her family took a lot of courage and I respect and love her for that. Maybe that's why I didn't completely write her off as a crazy lady when, toward the end of my eighth grade year and during my parents' separation, she called my brothers and me up to her room and said, "I've decided we're moving to Mexico."

NOTE

1. *Dumbo*, directed by Ben Sharpsteen (Burbank, California: Walt Disney Pictures, 1941), DVD.

The intensive Spanish class I attended in Mexico. The teacher was also the musical director.

4

INSTANT IMMERSION

We moved to Mexico mainly for one reason:

My mom wanted to learn a foreign language.

They say complete immersion is the best way to learn another language, right? So what could be better than just picking up and moving to the country that speaks the language you want to learn? Actually, I can think of a few ways to learn Spanish that would be much easier than uprooting an entire family and moving, but none of them would make nearly as good of a story and none of them would have given me the freedom to explore my own interests.

I thought my mom was joking when she told us she wanted to move our family to Mexico. Were we entering the witness protection program or something? Learning a foreign language had always been a goal of my mom's, but she had never had the time to pursue it so she figured this was as good a time as any.

Amid the stress of the separation, she began praying for the opportunity to move somewhere she could learn a new language and, fewer than twenty-four hours later, met a specialist at her school whose job was to help teachers teach students whose native language was something other than English.

Ms. Whetten introduced herself and asked, "Is there anything I can do to help you teach your Spanish-speaking students?" Almost facetiously, my mom replied, "Sure, find me a job in Mexico so I can learn to speak Spanish so I can communicate with my students and their parents." To my mother's surprise, Ms. Whetten, a native of Colonia Juarez, Chihuahua, Mexico, told her she could pretty much guarantee her a teaching job in the elementary school there. Less than a week later, my mother was booking tickets for our spring break to fly to Colonia Juarez, a small town of about a thousand people in the northern part of Mexico. It was settled by American Mormon pioneers in the late 1880s, and is still a thriving town to this day. A town in Mexico set-

BE CAREFUL WHAT YOU PRAY FOR! ;)

tled by Americans meant the majority of people were bilingual in Spanish and English, with most people having English as their native language.

I think my mom saw this as an opportunity for a fresh start, and so did I. Up to this point, I was still struggling a lot from my anxieties and the idea of moving to Mexico sparked some excitement I hadn't felt for a while. I wanted anything in my life that would allow me to feel like an ordinary kid again, and moving to Mexico seemed like it would be extraordinary.

Once we decided on going, my parents' divorce was finalized in just six weeks. My mom told me that was a miracle, because things like that usually don't happen that fast. I didn't know whether to be happy or sad about that, but I didn't really have the energy to worry about it . . . I was really sensitive to it still. I tried to occupy my mind with other things, but in doing so I realized this shocking truth: I was about to move to Mexico, and I only knew three Spanish words: *taco, burrito,* and *baño*."

WAKE UP EVERY DAY READY TO START A NEW ADVENTURE

As excited as I was to move to another country and get a new start on life, there was a little hesitancy in moving away from the friends I had made and the things I loved. One of the biggest things I was going to miss was American football. Even after my traumatic experience after practice when I was thirteen, I kept playing because it gave me a chance to release a lot of the stresses in my life *and* have fun at the same time. From the little I had learned about Mexico in school, I knew American football probably wasn't going to be around. I voiced my concerns to my mom's friend who was from Colonia Juarez, and she informed me that the high school I would be attending had an American football team. That's all I needed to hear. I was ready to leave that very day.

It was almost as if all the frustrations of my past were already being replaced by opportunities and *new* memories. Everything seemed to be falling into place. This was going to be the perfect chance for me to start fresh and hopefully return back to being the confident kid that had gotten lost in my anxiety.

As we loaded all our belongings into our ugly green van, I was bursting with excitement. We were moving a month early so I could join in football practices and I knew that would keep me occupied while I got used to the country.

As we left our Utah home in the distance, I took a good look around me. I had my family, I was about to embark on a once-in-lifetime experience while still getting to play the sport I loved, and my brother and I even figured out a way to set up a TV in the back of our van, so we could watch movies the entire seventeen hour road trip. Things were looking up.

Logan, Utah, was soon replaced by the desert and brush of New Mexico. The hours stretched on until we finally drove through El Paso and entered another desert parted only by the black stripe of the road we traveled. Three hours later we entered Colonia Juarez, which actually resembled nearly any small town I could imagine in Utah. Like I said, nearly everyone in Colonia Juarez spoke English and most of them were even members of the same church as me, so it really wasn't much different than living in Utah either—that first month anyway.

COLONIA JUAREZ

After getting settled in, we found out football didn't start a month early so instead of having to plan around practice schedules for a month, it meant I had time to adjust to my new city and make friends before school started in August. And it turns out that I had the best time that month. There was so much to do in Colonia Juarez—from swimming and hiking to paintballing in abandoned pig farms. It felt like there was never a shortage of things to do. It was like the world's best Scout camp, except I got to go home every night and sleep in my own bed. Also, since my brother Stephen and I shared a room together, there was never a dull moment at home. One memory that is always fresh on my mind is when we would lip-synch to Weird Al Yankovic's "The Saga Begins" before going to bed.

The rest of the summer our family met people at church and we were introduced to all of our neighbors. We even found out we had the perfect neighborhood gathering place right next to our house.

NOTE TO FUTURE SELF:
IF YOU EVER HAVE
THE CHANCE TO WORK
WITH WEIRD AL,
MAKE SURE YOU TELL
HIM THAT STORY.

There was a huge weeping willow in our yard that created a lot of shade and people would stop there all through the day and visit with each other. That was the perfect way to get to know everyone around. It wasn't long before I felt like I was quite a pro at living in Mexico. My new friends would meet up with me under that tree and we'd take our skateboards out to see the town and get tacos from street vendors. Of course, my friends would translate for me when I needed it, but I still didn't feel pressure to learn Spanish, so living there was easy.

I figured if I felt as familiar with the people in town as I did to people back home in Utah, then going to school shouldn't be much different than the American schools I was used to either. I psyched myself up for the first day and even convinced myself I could go to the school alone. Even if the office staff didn't speak English for whatever reasons, my friends would be close by to help. Besides, my mom needed to get her things ready to start teaching the next week and I didn't want to start ninth grade with my mom dragging me there.

School, like living in Colonia Juarez, was going to be a breeze.

I PROBABLY SHOULD HAVE LEARNED SPANISH

The first day of school was a lot different than I expected. More people attended than just those I'd gotten to know in my neighborhood. Of the four hundred students that attended, only about one hundred fifty were fluent in both Spanish and

English. The rest of them knew as much English as I knew Spanish. I figured the office staff and teachers would have to be fluent in English in order to work at a school with so many bilingual students, but I quickly learned that was not the case.

That was hard. I mean, the first day of school I was standing there in the office, trying to ask for my schedule and all they could do was stare. I did my best with charades, but how do you communicate an entire school schedule with a simple game of charades? How do you act out trying to find your history class when you know nothing about the history of the country you are currently in?

What's worse is that my friends were all busy trying to find their own classes. They were supposed to be my translators. They had been to this point—every time we went to the store or ran into someone who didn't speak English.

The five-minutes-until-class bell rang and I still didn't have my schedule. The feeling of anxiety was starting to kick in. What was taking this lady so long? Maybe she didn't speak English, but she should at least be able find a name in a computer and print off the schedule, no matter how American sounding the name was. After a minute or two I heard the printer start up. She took the paper off the tray and handed it to me. "Here go," she said. I think she was trying to say "Here *you* go." Or maybe she was just trying to get me to leave the office.

The page was still warm from the printer as I ran outside to my group of friends. It gave me a sense of relief when I saw some of my English speaking friends standing at the bottom of the stairs near the office. I said "hi" and was just about to ask them which building my first class was in when the class-is-starting bell rang. It was like a scene in a movie. All of the sudden, anyone that was still outside, including my two friends, bolted toward their respective buildings, leaving me alone outside. I stood there on the steps looking out at a completely empty campus.

I had no idea what to do. I looked at my schedule, trying to make some sense of it, but to no avail. I wandered around the campus looking for some type of clue to the building that connected with my schedule, but I couldn't see anything. Already, almost ten minutes late for class, I went back to the office to see if someone could help me. The only person available to offer assistance was the same lady who helped me get my schedule. It didn't matter if I spoke fast or slow, loud or soft, she didn't understand English. Bless her soul, but I was not up for playing another game of charades, especially with how stressed I was feeling right then.

Panic was rising. The anxiety I'd been learning to handle started to pulse back in, threatening me. I thought I'd been handling my anxiety pretty well up until then. I mean, the fact that I'd gone to the school alone proved I was getting better. But standing there paralyzed, unable to communicate with anyone, I thought it would *all* come back.

Now, twenty minutes late for my first class, on my first day of school, I went outside and plopped down on the steps of the main office building. I realized that if I was in the United States, this wouldn't have happened. That meant there was only one logical thing to do next. I needed to go to a place where people could understand me.

That's when I made up my mind. If I couldn't find my way to class, I'd go home. That was it. I just needed to go home. I was not talking about my home in Mexico either. I was talking about the home we'd left a month before. The place I called home was in the United States, where everyone spoke English.

I stood up from the steps, brushed myself off, and started the ten-minute walk back to our house to tell my mom I couldn't handle it and I wanted her to take me back to the United States. I was sure she would understand and be more than happy to take me back. My anxiety began creeping up on me when I began to think what I would do if she said no. There was no way I was staying here another day, so I began to plot my return trip in my mind. It seemed as if we'd driven for about three hours from the time we left El Paso, Texas, until we arrived in our new city of Colonia Juarez. Based on my calculations, it couldn't possibly take more than a day by foot to get to El Paso because by car the trip was approximately three hours. That's all I'd need is to get back to El Paso because I could call my grandparents from there and they'd figure out how to come get me. People would understand me in El Paso, and that would make me a lot more comfortable.

Cell phones had been introduced by now but I didn't have the luxury of owning one just yet so I couldn't Google the distance from Colonia Juarez to El Paso. If I had, I'd have known it was more than three days walk, and that was without stopping once for a break.

JUST TRY ONE MORE DAY

Once I got home, I squared my shoulders and walked in my front door.

"Stuart, what are you doing home?" my mom asked as I stood just inside the front door.

I steadied myself and said, "I want to go home, and if you won't take me, I will walk there."

"You can't walk all the way home," she said.

"I don't need to walk *all* the way there. I only need to make it as far as the border and then Grandma can pick me up. You don't have to do anything."

I must not have been too bad of a child because my mother didn't volunteer to help me pack.

"Take me back home. I don't want to do this," I said.

CHAPTER 4

"I don't know if that's the best thing to do right now," she said.

I shook my head. I couldn't talk to *anyone*. Football didn't begin when it should have and now I'd have to travel *hours* to every single game. School had turned into a disaster and I had no idea what had happened to any of my friends in that building. Looking at my life in that moment, I just couldn't see any way things would work out for me.

"I'm out of here. I don't care. I'm *walking* home," I declared.

I think she realized how serious I was, because she stopped what she was doing and gave me her full attention. I could tell she was thinking about what she should say. Probably because she knew that if she didn't give a good enough answer, I really would start the journey back to the border. My mom looked at me with this expression that meant *don't argue, this is just advice, but advice you need to follow nonetheless*, and said, "I think you should try one more day. Go to school one more day and you can decide tomorrow if you still want to go home. If tomorrow you still want to go home, we can talk about it then."

My mother is either a great motivator or an expert manipulator. Perhaps she's a bit of each, because somehow, I found the courage to walk back to the school alone. I thought hard about my future with every single step. I wouldn't be able to continue here without at least trying to learn Spanish. I had to learn how to communicate, and I really didn't know how hard that was going to be for me. I also had to try and make more friends. I'd need people in my classes to help me through the year.

Once I made it back to the school, I found one of my classrooms, and to my relief, most of the kids in the class were the friends I'd made in my neighborhood, the ones who spoke English! That was a huge help, because in that particular school, we moved from class to class with the same group of kids all year long. Being with my friends in that one class meant I'd be with them the entire day, every day. I was relieved at the thought that I'd be able to communicate with nearly everyone in all of my classes. I can't even describe the relief that flowed through me as I sat at my desk and took inventory of all the kids I could communicate with.

About this time I learned an important fact:

School in Mexico was out to get me.

About a week into the school year, I got called to the office and was told that, starting that day, they would be transferring me into a different class group with a Spanish hour that was the same time as the beginning Spanish class. That meant when they went to advanced Spanish, I would go to my beginning Spanish class and then rejoin them after. I wasn't bugged at all. In fact, I loved the idea of getting some extra help on my Spanish. I left the office and headed to a different classroom to meet my new peers. As I opened the door to the class my heart sunk. There was only one native English speaking student in the class. Matters were only made worse when I found out that half of the teachers for this group didn't speak English, which was strange since nearly everyone in the town of Colonia Juarez was bilingual.

I thought briefly about sneaking over the border, but my mom had done a great job at convincing me that first day of school to give it a little more time.

Of course my friends continued on in their classes, able to communicate with one another, while I was left to ask myself one recurring question:

Why had I taken *French* in middle school?

*Some of my fellow sailors and me in the our
school production of* South Pacific.

5

I'M AN ACTOR!

I gave up on my plans to sneak across the border into El Paso once I got over the shock of my first couple weeks of school in Mexico.

I walked to school each morning, went to every class, and stared at the words on the chalkboard that everyone could read but me. I listened to each teacher speak in a language that made as much sense to me as radio static. I was a thirteen-year-old boy. How could they put me through this? Wasn't there some law against putting kids in classes where they couldn't understand things? If not, I would be the first to vote in favor of it. My mom's counsel was still fresh on my mind, so I decided I was here to stay, and I'd better make the most of the year. That determination helped me start having a little fun. As optimistic as I was about the future, I still didn't believe what our neighbor Vonnie had said when we first moved in. She was this cute, vivacious grandma-type neighbor. As she was standing under our willow tree, fanning herself in the shade, she said, "Are you sure you want to live here? Because most people who move here don't ever want to leave."

Her expression was a mixture of concern and teasing. I didn't say it out loud, but I could never imagine myself staying there forever, nor ever wanting to. I was here for a year only, and with the struggle to learn Spanish, I decided that was all the time I'd need to be ready to go back home.

After only a few weeks of living in Mexico, I'd already made this startling discovery:

Being a minority was pretty tough.

> **NEVER FORGET WHAT IT FELT LIKE TO BE THE ONE ON THE OUTSIDE.**

LONGING TO BELONG

About three months into the school year, I was still struggling with the culture shock of living in another country, no matter how Americanized the town was. I still felt very alone so I prayed for an opportunity to make some more friends and feel more like I belonged somewhere. One day after school, I saw a lot of my friends huddled around the door of a classroom looking at a list with some names on it. I got closer and saw it was the cast list for the school musical, *South Pacific*. As I scanned through the sheet, the names of many of my English-speaking friends stood out to me and I wished I could be in the play with them. How I longed to get back on a stage in front of people. I really hadn't had any chances to do that since leaving Utah.

"Why didn't I hear about this?" I asked the kid next to me.

A friend of mine was walking by just then and stopped. "You could go talk to the director to see if you can still get a part," he said.

I had never been in a musical or play before, but I remember thinking, *No. That's not how things work. You don't just "walk on" in musicals.* But even as I was thinking that, I had this feeling that I should just go and talk to the director anyway. This would probably be the only shot I would have at some sort of a social life during my freshman year.

It was a little out of my comfort zone, but as I thought about it some more, I knew I needed to try. That little voice in my heart was getting easier to recognize and I couldn't put it off.

I pushed the nervousness down to my gut and made the walk to the school auditorium. As I entered the performance hall doors, I saw the director, instructing some of my friends on stage.

Great, I thought. *They've already started rehearsing. There's no way she'll let me join now.*

There was a small break where the director sat down.

It's now or never, I thought.

I approached the director and mumbled, "I just saw the cast list. I was wondering if there was a way I could still be part of the play?"

She looked at me like, "We already *had* tryouts." Her expression made me want to sulk away, but I waited, anxious for her response. The play was all in English so that wouldn't be an issue, but I hadn't gone to tryouts . . .

She just stared at me, looking me up and down without making a sound. I wondered for a minute if I'd made a serious mistake in approaching her, but her expression softened and she said, "Yes. I think we can find a spot for you."

A feeling of joy came over me. A feeling I had been longing to feel. I'm so grateful for that director for giving me a chance to perform. I think she could see that there was something inside of me that needed that experience. It was more than simply being in a play. I believe it's what saved me that year in Mexico. It not only gave me a purpose, but it provided me with a chance to be with friends and to develop a new talent.

> *WHATEVER YOUR SITUATION, FIND A PURPOSE IN IT.*

A SAILOR IN SOUTH PACIFIC

My role as a sailor in *South Pacific* was my first acting "job" and it gave me something to look forward to every day.

It seriously filled me with joy, and I fell in love again with performing. Even though this was totally different than my first magic trick in the fifth grade talent show, it was me being part of something bigger. It was me being able to entertain.

Practice was in full swing and I enjoyed every minute of it. Our high school version of *South Pacific* was a good, clean version of the play. But then again, I'd never seen the original, so I had no idea how much our production differed from the Hollywood version. I only had one small line and was included as a backup singer in the chorus most of the time. None of this mattered though, I was just glad to be part of it.

It really taught me to look at performing from a creative point of view, standing there on that stage in a sailor's costume, listening to the lines while trying to imagine what the audience would see. Would they notice my individual movements while they were watching the lead character? Even if they didn't notice my acting skills, they would certainly notice if I stood up on stage and did nothing. That's one thing

> *HAVE YOU EVER THOUGHT THAT MAYBE OUR EXPERIENCES DON'T HAPPEN BY COINCIDENCE BUT ARE ORCHESTRATED FOR OUR OWN GOOD?*

that made this experience so interesting. Each of us alone was almost insignificant, yet together we were part of a bigger picture. Together we made it work, but if any one of us didn't pull his or her weight, it would be obvious to those coming to be entertained.

LIVE ON STAGE

After months of rehearsals, we finally performed *South Pacific*. Our first performance was a matinee showing for the local elementary school. We watched through the curtains as they all filed into the high school auditorium. I thought back to my elementary school days and how excited I was to see the high school students perform. I wondered if I might inspire someone through my performance that day.

The first act started and I could already tell it was going to be rough. Everyone kept messing up their lines and missing their cues. Worst of all, I could tell the audience was not understanding the story line. Intermission could not come soon enough. When the last note was sung at the end of the first act, we all huddled up backstage and received a positive pep talk from our director. I really hoped we could do better. . . . I didn't want to let those kids down. Determined to perform better in the second act, we returned to the main stage to get into position only to discover the curtain was open and our entire audience was gone. I couldn't believe it.

The director was there with us, looking at the empty seats. We probably stared out into the empty auditorium for a full minute when the director finally vocalized the numbing truth. "They just left," she said.

Luckily, we all managed to have a positive attitude, viewing this as a learning experience that was challenging us to do better in the performances to follow. Most of the shows after that went off without a hitch . . . except for the night of our final performance.

A SAILOR WITH A CELL PHONE

All the sailors were about to walk on stage for one of our biggest scenes of the first act. Right as we were walking on, one of the sailors realized he had his cell phone in hand. Thinking quickly, he kind of slid his phone underneath a platform by the backdrop on stage. *Whew. Good save*, I thought. But I was still confused why he didn't just put it in his pocket.

Two minutes into the scene, his phone started to ring. The sound carried throughout the entire auditorium. There we were, trying to say our lines and carry on like there wasn't a phone ringing under the backdrop. I could feel the awkwardness in the room and just wished the call would stop. Whomever was calling this kid must have really wanted to get a hold of him, because the phone immediately started ringing a second time. That was the most awkward performance of my life.

As bad as those performances were, we had some good nights in between, even a few where the entire auditorium was full. By the time we performed for the last time, nearly everyone in Colonia Juarez had seen the show. But it wasn't the final result that made the biggest impact on me, it was the overall experience of performing in *South Pacific* that changed my life. It was learning to perform on stage, set goals, and have a purpose. It was the connection I felt every time I stood in front of people and offered them some form of entertainment.

ADJUSTING IS A PROCESS

The anxiety of not being able to communicate eased as I began to learn simple Spanish phrases. My scores even improved in Spanish class, so I had actual proof of my improvement.

Don't get me wrong. I still had struggles. I couldn't communicate very effectively and I was still adjusting to life as the oldest child in a single-parent home. But as time passed, I began to see the good in life again. I began helping my mom with my younger brothers and taking care of them when the power went out or when they were struggling with their own trials. I guess you could say I was actually growing up.

OVERCOMING ANXIETY

Of all the experiences I had during my time as a teenager in Mexico, I'm most grateful that I was eventually able to manage my anxiety. I don't know much about the medical or psychological side of anxiety caused by traumatic experiences, but somehow I

DON'T EVER UNDERESTIMATE THE JOY YOU CAN FEEL BY SPENDING QUALITY TIME WITH YOUR FAMILY.

was able to deal with it. I know there are some of you reading this book that may be struggling with something similar to what I went through, so I would like to share my experience with how I dealt with those stresses.

I conquered anxiety by retraining my brain. When anxiety would start to arise, I would ask myself a series of questions about possible outcomes. I would throw out the most outrageous outcomes, because their chances of happening were highly unlikely, and force myself to think about the most probable outcome. If I was worried about being away from my mom, I would think, *What's the worst that could happen?* Usually I would come to the conclusion that the worst thing that could happen would be that while I was away, she got in an accident and died. I would reassure myself that it wasn't very likely to happen, and if for some reason it did, I would be sad but would eventually be able to cope with it. It wasn't always easy, but it made each new experience easier to confront.

That's not to say I spent every moment in Mexico worrying whether I would shortly lose someone I loved. I went paintballing, traveled with the sports teams, experienced a few crushes on girls, learned to play the guitar, laughed with my friends, and overall, just had a lot of fun.

I even made my first real video in Mexico.

The assistant wrestling coach giving me a few pointers in between matches at a tournament.

6

NEVER QUIT

My friend Ethan and I decided to enter a video into a competition put on by our school's seminary program. Since seminary is the study of religion, the video had to focus on a Bible story. We chose Noah.

I've already explained how I feel when I entertain people on stage, and I learned it isn't much different when I entertain people with videos.

I simply felt free to create, as if nothing could hold me back.

I played Noah and Ethan played the person banging on the door of the ship, begging to be let in after the rain began. Once we had it all filmed, we used Ethan's dad's computer to edit it all together and burn it to a CD for our teacher.

I loved watching the editing process and I wanted to edit my own movies. Making movies would incorporate everything I had realized I wanted to do in life: I would be entertaining, I would be taking on different roles, and I would be making people smile. The idea even ran through my head that it would be fun to make and edit videos for a living, but as soon as the thought entered, doubt dismissed it.

I saw an impossible path to film. My reasoning was pretty straightforward, and at the time it made perfect sense. In order to be a filmmaker, I would have to work for someone else so I could learn the business and make a living. That meant I'd have to promote their ideas and themes, which may or may not be something I believed in, and I never wanted to get involved in a film that didn't uphold my morals.

So even though I loved watching Ethan edit our little video, I couldn't justify working in an environment where I would have to film or edit by someone else's standards, especially when they may be vastly different than my own. At only thirteen years old, I had found something I wanted to follow, but had to eliminate it from my career path because I was certain it would compromise my standards.

> NEVER GIVE UP ON SOMETHING YOU'RE PASSIONATE ABOUT. IF YOU WANT IT BADLY ENOUGH, AND WORK HARD ENOUGH FOR IT, A WAY WILL OPEN UP FOR YOU TO ACCOMPLISH IT.

YOUTUBE'S DEBUT

Shortly after I made my decision to never get into filmmaking, a group of PayPal employees became increasingly frustrated that there was no easy way to share videos online. It was 2003 and there was no real platform to support *independent* filmmakers, actors, or musicians. At the time, all you could really do with film was work for a big company, making the films *they* wanted to make, containing content *they* wanted. There was no way to create your own films or short videos and actually distribute them.

Those PayPal employees weren't necessarily filmmakers; they were just interested in seeing other people's videos of world events and life experiences. So they came up with this crazy idea to create a video-sharing website, called it YouTube, and uploaded the first test video called "Me at the Zoo."

YouTube went viral.

Within a short time, sixty-five thousand new videos were being uploaded to YouTube every day, attracting the attention of viewers and filmmakers around the world. A few years later YouTube introduced their advertising programs. Advertisers could purchase ad space on the YouTube page or on actual videos. It proved quite successful to place ads on popular videos, and more advertisers jumped on board. The YouTube team once again revolutionized the online video world when they decided to split advertising revenue with the video's creators. Whether they'd intended to or not, those founders were revolutionizing the video industry while I was living in the dry deserts of Mexico, singing songs about the South Pacific.

EVEN THOUGH THERE ARE MANY VIDEO-SHARING WEBSITES NOW ONLINE, YOUTUBE IS STILL #1. IN FACT, YOUTUBE HAS BECOME MORE POPULAR THAN TELEVISION.

There was no way for me to know it then, but what those guys started back in 2003 would change my life profoundly.

TIME TO GO HOME

I'm grateful for that time in Mexico when I developed a love for music and for new cultures. But the most valuable thing for me was that I developed a deep understanding of acceptance and self-discovery.

When the time came for us to return to the United States, Vonnie's prediction came true. I didn't want to leave, but my mom's sabbatical was up and it was time to return to our "real life" in Utah.

We loaded everything into our ugly green van and drove away from our Colonia Juarez home. For this drive, we had upgraded our old TV into a cool little portable DVD player. The only DVD we had at the time was *Napoleon Dynamite*. I remember replaying the dance scene he does for the school assembly over and over again, each time laughing so hard I cried.

Even though we returned to the same area in Utah, we lived in different school boundaries than before. It wasn't hard to get used to being back, it hardly felt like I'd been living in a different country anyway, it was just hard to start a new school with new people once again.

By the time fall came, I was ready to begin my sophomore year in high school. Since I'd finally learned to speak Spanish in Mexico, I was able to jump right into advanced Spanish my sophomore year. That really impressed the girls at school. And since I'd fallen in love with acting in Mexico, it was only natural to sign up for the high school play, *Hello Dolly*. I learned my lesson this time and made sure to actually audition. I wasn't sure if all directors would be as nice as the one in Mexico.

There were lots of kids from my neighborhood in *Hello Dolly*, so I was able to interact with them and I made lots of friends.

Along with acting, I also jumped into a new sport:

Wrestling.

YOU'LL PASS OUT BEFORE YOU DIE

Wrestling was huge for me. I started wrestling at a time in my life where I needed discipline and, boy, did I get it. The discipline I learned from wrestling has continued to help me push through hard times, helping me stick to my goals. Every day after classes I was being disciplined by my coach and held to a high standard. He expected greatness, and because of that, I also began to expect it of myself.

> YOU'VE GOT TO FIND A PURPOSE, BUT THEN YOU'VE GOT TO MAKE SURE YOU HAVE THE DISCIPLINE TO STICK WITH IT.

Anyone that's ever wrestled will tell you how hard practices can be. They are tough. I mean *really* tough. One thing my coach would always say to us as he was pushing us to what we thought was our physical limits was, "Don't worry— you'll pass out before you die." . . . As if that was supposed to comfort us, knowing that no matter how hard the workout was, we wouldn't just die right there on the mat—we'd pass out first. Even though it was an absurd phrase, and I would have loved to prove him wrong on it, it still motivated me to push myself to my limits and see what I was capable of achieving, both physically and emotionally.

IF YOU WIN, IT'S OVER

Toward the end of my second year wrestling, our team competed in an elimination-style tournament against all the schools in our area. It was the third period of my first round and I was taken by surprise by my opponent. He grabbed me from behind and threw me sideways. I lost my balance and tried to catch myself as I crashed down on my right arm.

A shaft of pain shot through my shoulder and I wondered for just a second if I should tap out and end the match. Despite the pain, I decided I couldn't work this hard all year and go out on the first round. I was ahead in points, so I got up and just circled around as much as I could until the referee finally blew the whistle. I won the match by default, which meant I moved on to the next round. My coaches asked me if everything was fine and I didn't tell them anything about my shoulder. I thought if I let them know I was injured I wouldn't be able to wrestle anymore and I didn't want all my practice to go to waste.

After a small break, I was back on the mat for my second match. At the sound of the whistle, my opponent immediately shot in and took me down. I landed square on my right shoulder again. I wiggled around and broke myself free from my opponent and stood up on the mat. The referee asked if I was okay and gave me a quick second to catch my breath. I came here to have fun today and subjecting myself to a constant shoulder beating wasn't proving to be enjoyable. I just wanted to get off that mat as quickly as possible. In a split second I realized I had three options to end that match: I could give up, I could let him pin me, or I could pin him. I liked the third option and realized that, the sooner I pinned my opponent, the sooner the match would be over. I think my opponent could sense I was getting psyched up about something, because I could tell he was getting antsy. Or maybe it was because I gave him this look that said something like, "I'm about to take you down so hard. Don't worry though . . . you'll pass out before you die."

We made our way to the center and the ref gave us the signal to continue. Disregarding the pain in my shoulder, I shot in on my opponent as hard as I could, knowing that the faster I pinned the kid, the sooner I'd be off the mat. I got a solid hold on him, picked him up, and took him straight to the ground. He hit pretty hard, and I locked him up and rolled him onto his shoulders. *Thweeeeeet!* The referee blew his whistle signaling a pin had happened and the match was over.

I shook hands with my opponent and approached the sideline to wait for my next match. My opponent in the third match put up more of a fight, but the second he opened himself up too much, I shot in, locked him up, and threw his shoulders right into the mat. The ref blew his whistle and I barely waited for him to announce me the winner before I was back on the sideline.

> **"BEING CHALLENGED IN LIFE IS INEVITABLE; BEING DEFEATED IS OPTIONAL."**
> **—ROGER CRAWFORD**

As the championship round came around I didn't think I could do it anymore. I was absolutely beat, but I'd gotten this far, and there was no point in giving up now. I walked onto the mat to face my opponent. This guy was huge. We were both in the 152 weight class, but they must have gotten the scales messed up because this guy looked more like 251. He towered over me as we shook hands and the referee blew the whistle.

He immediately shot in and wrapped a hold of my legs. His arms seriously felt like vice grips as he picked me up and threw me onto my right shoulder. Pain shot through the entire right side of my body. I fought free, but it wasn't long before he was throwing me back to the mat. I felt like a wild gazelle being tossed around by a hungry lion. I had lost all strength. Every time I tried to get up, he would throw me back down onto my hurt shoulder. Had someone tipped him off that my shoulder was hurt? I was furious. I was furious, I was so exhausted, and I was sure I would die. I was so exhausted, I thought I would die. Maybe today would be the day that my coach was proved wrong—you actually can die on the mat without passing out first.

After what felt like hours of constant struggling, I finally heard the referee's whistle. It wasn't to signal the end of the period, but that I had been pinned. I don't remember how I was pinned or even when it happened. I was so beat from the other matches, I just couldn't remember.

I got second place that day in the tournament. But the lesson I learned was more important than the medal I earned. I learned quitting isn't the only option to get something over with. Sometimes the best way to get through a tough time, is to win, and win fast. What my coach yelled at us every practice has stuck with me all these years. Even though I still think his motivation tactics were a little crazy, he was right in saying that sometimes when you think you've given all you can give, there's always a little gas left in the tank that can get you through it.

That life lesson would come in handy for me when I returned to Mexico, this time walking the desert streets . . . for two years.

Let's just say I walked a lot as a missionary.

7

CALLED TO SERVE

In 2007, I graduated from high school. The most important thing you need to know about my high school experience was that I learned that I loved ballroom dancing, playing the guitar, and God. Shortly after graduating, I started preparing to serve as a full-time missionary for my church. It's not uncommon for the girls and guys in my church to willingly devote a year and a half to two years of their lives as volunteer missionaries, teaching people around the world about God. Some go right at the age of eighteen, while others wait and go a little later. For those of you who are unfamiliar with missions, I'll explain them a little for you.

The young men in our church are encouraged to give two years of their life teaching and serving people around the world, all at their own expense, meaning it's not a paid ministry. We fill out the proper paperwork, are interviewed by our leaders to determine our worthiness, and then are assigned a location in which to serve—which could be anywhere around the world speaking any language.

We believe God has a hand in all if it, sending us to places where we have unique abilities and talents to help the people in that area. We're informed of our mission details, or "mission call" through a letter from the church headquarters. Whether we choose to accept our assignment, we send back a letter stating as such, and then, before going out to our assigned area, we go to one of the many Missionary Training Centers around the world for a period of anywhere from two to six weeks. (The length of a missionary's stay is dependent on the language he or she is learning. The average stay is about two or three weeks though.)

Because our time as a missionary is so valuable, we follow rules and schedules designed to help us eliminate distractions and keep us focused on our purpose as missionaries, which is to invite others to come unto Christ. We're told which areas to work in and we're assigned a *companion* (of the same gender) so that together our message can be strengthened. Companions also hold each other accountable. And we do all of this willingly. No one is holding us out there against our will. I will confess, however, when I first got my mission call and read that I had been called to serve in Veracruz, Mexico, I was kind of disappointed. *Mexico? I've already been to Mexico . . .* Had I mixed up the "Countries I've lived in" and "Countries I would like to serve in" columns in the mission application? (Not sure if they still have that option.) However I quickly felt confirmation that Veracruz, Mexico, was where God could best use me.

SHARING THE GOSPEL IN VERACRUZ

A quick Google search revealed that Veracruz is located on the Gulf of Mexico, almost the complete opposite side of the country from where I lived when I was fourteen.

Veracruz is hot, humid, and home to mangoes and many types of scorpions and spiders. I like mangoes. I hate spiders.

In one of my first areas, my companion and I felt we should swing home for a second after lunch. Upon arriving home we saw a tarantula scurry across the floor. I froze in my tracks. I'm convinced had we not gone home when we did, we would have never seen the spider and it would have eaten me alive in my sleep. Okay . . . maybe I'm being a bit dramatic.

I could share countless experiences about the things I learned while serving as a missionary, but for the sake of this book, I will keep it simple.

As I began my mission in Veracruz, much of the life was familiar, but a lot of it was drastically different than anything I'd seen or experienced before. The streets were filthy, the heat unbearable, and raw sewage flowed through the city in these nasty ditches to wherever it was they processed the stuff. I learned a lot of valuable life lessons as a missionary. For example, if a drunk man with a machete doesn't want to be talked to, you should probably just leave him alone. I also learned that when you're hastily walking to an appointment, make sure you are watching your surroundings or you might just happen to fall knee-deep in sewage water.

I know these near-death experiences make it sound like being a missionary is the best thing ever (yes, I would classify falling in sewage as a near-death experience), but rest assured, missions are more than just fun and games. For me it was one of the first times I was really out on my own, and I realized I had the power make my own decisions.

WHEN EVERYTHING CHANGED

Like I mentioned earlier, we always work in teams of two on our missions. We set goals and teach lessons together, share our life stories with one another, bunk together, hold each other accountable, and watch out for each other. Companion transfers happened every six weeks. Although that didn't necessarily mean you would get a new companion every transfer. Usually you are with a companion for three to four months. Most of the time, companionships get along pretty well, but, as you'd expect, putting two nineteen-year-old young men in a small one-bedroom apartment with two beds and not allowing them to leave each other's sight, twenty-four hours a day, seven days a week, could lead to a little head butting. I definitely had my fair share of head butts.

At one point, nearly a year into my mission, I wasn't getting along with my assigned companion. We came from completely different cultures, so we just didn't see eye-to-eye on a lot of things. The area we were assigned to cover was "Las Bajadas" Its literal English translation is "The Dumps," and that's exactly what is was. It was so hot and dirty and there were only one or two paved roads in the entire area. Dirt roads I would have been okay with, but being only a few miles from the ocean, the roads were made of sand that got in the cracks of our shoes and into our socks, making it really uncomfortable to walk.

Since we were always outside, there was a time when our mission leader's wife told all the missionaries to make sure we wore sunscreen. We wanted to be obedient to the instructions given to us, so every morning, before heading out, we put on the thick, greasy SPF 50 and then went to work.

The sunscreen was awful! It caked on our faces and itched all day long because it produced even more sweat than we were already battling. Sometimes we would get a gust of wind, but instead of it being a cool refreshing breeze, it was a hot blast of sandy air. I seriously wondered if a sunburn might be more comfortable.

One morning we woke up and got ready for the long day ahead. We slathered on our sunscreen, left our apartment, and nearly melted in the scalding heat. We looked at our appointment book only to realize that it was completely empty. We had nobody to teach.

CHAPTER 7

WHY AM I HERE?

I was the senior companion, so I felt a huge responsibility to make sure we stayed busy, but I seriously had no idea where to start. I looked at my companion and asked, "Where do think we should go?" He just shrugged his shoulders like he always did whenever I asked for his input on something. Couldn't he at least say something? Even if he'd said, "Let's just go back inside and sleep," I would have at least entertained the idea and been grateful he had suggested something for us to do.

Not knowing where to go combined with my companion's silence regarding the matter was getting too much for me to handle. At that moment, an obnoxiously loud city bus sped by sending a cloud of dust right at us. The sunscreen on my face that I was so *obediently wearing* was now dripping into my eyes. I gave into frustration and just plopped down on the curb. Slouched over with my head bowed, I wondered why this was so hard. I was serving God, so shouldn't this be easy? Was it too much to ask for better weather or a companion that gave me his two cents instead of using it to buy Bubu Lubus (a Mexican chocolate marshmallow candy).

As I sat moping on the curb for what had been about a minute, the ugliest stray dog you could ever imagine, walked by and I watched as it meandered down the street.

Staring as that thing walked away, it hit me. No, not the dog . . . but a thought . . . *I'm in Mexico. I am literally in the dumps of Mexico, sitting on a curb, watching a homeless dog. Why am I even here?* If I wanted to, I could back go inside, sleep all day and no one would stop me. I could even return to the United States, with no consequences, to get back to a normal life, free from flea-infested stray dogs.

I thought about whether what I was doing was right for me and I came to the conclusion that, as hard as it was, I *did* want to be serving a mission. I loved that I had the opportunity to help so many people with selfless acts of service and I *was* grateful every day was filled with a new struggle that helped me grow. As I looked at my current situation though, staying inside seemed a lot more appealing. In that moment, the words popped into my head, "Fake it 'til you make it."

I repeated that phrase over and over in my mind for a few seconds . . . examining it from all different angles just to make sure it would actually be able to sustain me. It was as though I had been stranded on a deserted island and wanted make sure the life raft I just stumbled upon didn't have any unseen leaks or holes that might eventually leave me sinking out at sea. Starting to feel some motivation from the thought, but still not sure I'd be able to last long doing it, I got up and forced myself to move forward. My companion followed suit, probably thinking I had remembered someone we could go teach, but the truth is, I had no idea where I was going. I just knew that getting up and moving was a lot better than sitting down. The rest of the day I had to force myself to smile as we spoke to people. (I'm sorry to anyone I might have not given proper attention to during that time.) The first days of my new method were a little rigid and disingenuous, but, miraculously, pretty soon, I wasn't faking it anymore, I was making it. I was sincerely loving every experience I had, whether difficult or fun. My relationship with my companion was strengthened as well. I was transferred to a new area a few weeks later but we stayed great friends the rest of my mission.

WITH THE RIGHT ATTITUDE, YOU CAN MAKE IT THROUGH ANYTHING

I think that's when I started to realize my success depended first upon my own attitude about what I was doing. I decided I would be happy, or at least pretend to be until it became real. I would work harder and push forward as if I had a purpose every minute of the day. Even still today, I have moments where I need to force a smile and be happy when I'd much rather sit at home away from the world. Sometimes I just don't feel like taking a selfie or showing someone a magic trick. While we shouldn't force ourselves to be happy all the time (sometimes you just need to have a bad day), I think there are a lot of situations that would become bearable, even beneficial, if we would just change our attitude. Captain Jack Sparrow actually had some pretty good advice about facing hard times. He said, "The problem is not the problem. The problem is your attitude about the problem."[1]

THE BEST TWO YEARS?

At the end of my two-year mission, I was definitely a much better person than when I started. I was a harder worker, I had a solid moral compass, and I was finally able to eat cow stomach and keep it in my stomach.

Many people return home from serving their missions to proclaim that it was the best two years of their life. I think it's because a mission is all about serving others. It's about forgetting yourself and putting God's will first. It's about witnessing that change in others.

That certainly does make for a good two years, but I don't agree that those two years should always be labeled as your "best." And this isn't just applicable to missionary service, but any time we are doing anything that is laying a foundation for our life. You don't set out to build your dream home and then stop once the basement is laid and go, "Oh wow, look at these concrete walls! Aren't these the best?! You know what? I'm just going to move all my stuff in now and call it good." The foundation serves a crucial part to the entire home, but there are so many more essential and exciting things yet to be built on top of that.

If I'm always looking back to a past event as the "best time of my life" for the rest of my life, there must be something wrong. I have the potential to be happy; *you* have the potential to be happy. We should make each upcoming year the best year, week, or day we have ever had.

SOME FINAL THOUGHTS ON MISSIONARY SERVICE

I feel like there may be some of you reading this that might be in the same situation I was once in, or something similar to it. I feel it's important for me to mention that whether I had decided to serve a mission, I could have, and *would* have still been given experiences to help me learn, grow, and become a better person. Giving up my time to serve a mission was a sacrifice for me, and I know I was blessed and will continue to be blessed because of that. God blesses us when we have faith in Him, no matter how impossible it may seem to our mortal minds.

You are unique. I'm definitely unique. We have our own personalities, our own strengths, and even our own weaknesses. But that's what makes us good at what we do. I believe we all have specific callings here on earth—specific tasks to accomplish and specific lives to touch. Heavenly Father called me to serve a mission in Veracruz, Mexico, but when I returned, that did not mean my mission in life was over.

You may have a different mission on earth, but whatever it is, embrace it and love it.

NOTE

1. Johnny Depp, *Pirates of the Caribbean: The Curse of the Black Pearl*, directed by Gore Verbinski (Burbank, California: Walt Disney Pictures, 2003), DVD.

PART 2

IT ALL STARTS TO COME TOGETHER

8

LIFE IS FINALLY BEGINNING

A few weeks after returning home from my mission in Mexico, I moved to Provo, Utah. As exciting as it was to return home from being a full-time missionary and reunite with my family, I lay in bed my first night home thinking, *Oh wow. Life is starting now.*

You see, growing up, the only thing I really worried about was whether I would serve a mission someday. Now that I was back from my mission, I had to figure out what I wanted to do for the rest of my life. What career did I want to have? Where did I want to go to school? Who would I date? Better yet, who would I marry and start a family with?

I was getting overwhelmed with all these life decisions I felt I needed to be make in the near future. So I sought counsel from my mom.

She told me that while I was on my mission, the ballroom team at Utah Valley University (a college about two hours from my home)

> IT'S INTERESTING HOW SOME OF OUR MOST CRUCIAL LIFE DECISIONS ARE MADE AT A TIME IN OUR LIVES WHEN WE KNOW HARDLY ANYTHING.

had appeared on the TV show *Dancing with the Stars*. She knew how much I enjoyed my ballroom classes in high school and commented that if I went to school there and made the team maybe I could dance on the show. At first I thought she might be joking with me. Did she really just suggest that my first major life decision should be to decide whether I should be a ballroom dancer? I mean, I did enjoy dancing. As a matter of fact, when I was in high school I did think it would be cool if somehow, someday, I was able to be on that show. However, I knew I was definitely not a master of ballroom dance. As I pondered it some more, I realized it might not be that bad of an idea after all. I'd heard UVU was a quality school and that Provo was a great place for young single adults. There were tons of fun activities going on all the time. Plenty of people to meet, friends to make, and definitely plenty of girls to date. I had an uncle that taught at UVU, so I would have some family close by, and who knew, maybe I would make the dance team and find my calling in life . . . wearing shiny shoes and pants and shaking my booty on a dance floor.

FINDING THE RIGHT JOB

Earlier that summer, I'd found a job in Logan working as a Spanish/English translator at a local elementary school for the summer classes. I decided that I would leave the comfort of my home in Logan, if, and only if, I could find a similar job in Provo. I filled out nearly thirty applications for schools around the Provo area and only two called me back. One was for a teacher's aide position for a classroom of students ages six to eleven who were identified with individualized behavioral plans. The other was being an assistant in a classroom for adults with special needs. The latter required that I do a lot of heavy lifting and be willing to change diapers. I wasn't too sure I'd be able to handle that. So I picked the behavior classroom, thinking it would be easier to manage and not require as much energy from me. I had no idea, however, that my life was about to change drastically by the lessons I would learn in that classroom.

THE WISDOM OF KIDS

I packed all my belonging into my tiny blue Hyundai Accent and drove down to Provo, Utah. My new job was going to take up a lot more time than I anticipated, so I was unable to try out for the ballroom dance team. Regardless, I was happy I had moved to "Happy Valley."

Anyone that's been around kids knows that sometimes they can say the funniest yet most profound things. That was no exception with the kids I worked with.

The kids in that classroom were amazing. They were smart, caring, and curious about the world around them. They were outspoken, straight up honest, and tons of fun to work with. They also gave me some advice I'll never forget. That's one thing about kids—you don't even have to ask for it but you're going to get advice. You just have to figure out if it's helpful or if it's going to get you sent to the principal's office.

I KNOW *ALL* ABOUT HUMAN NATURE

One little girl made a particular impression on me. We'll call her Sara. She was seven years old and she was *tiny*. I mean, seriously, she was so small that her backpack was bigger than she was. If she put anything more than a single piece of paper in her backpack, she may not have been able to carry it. Even though Sara was small, she was smart and spunky, and *loved* to talk.

Mostly every day, I sat at a horseshoe shaped table in the back of the classroom and would be there to help a small group of students with their assignments for that day. One day, while we were working in a small group around the table, Sara nonchalantly asked, "Mr. Stuart, are you married?" She didn't raise her head, didn't look at me . . . nothing. Just asked the question and continued working on her assignment.

I took just a second to respond because Sara was always saying something off-the-wall—I wondered where this question would lead. "No. I'm not married," I said finally. As much as I wanted to hear her response, I needed her to be focused, so I tried to end it with one comment.

Her pencil just kept working its way across her paper, and I thought maybe for the first time that year, I was going to keep her on task, when all off the sudden— "That means you don't have a life," she said casually.

"Wait, what?" I said.

Working away on her assignment, she added, "It means you can't have a house or a car."

I could not wrap my mind around how she connected those two scenarios. I was no longer concerned with whether she stayed on task, I was just hoping for some sort of explanation on how she had come to that conclusion. The boy sitting next to her, Matthew, stopped working on his assignment and decided to join in. "I don't think that's true, Sara . . ."

Immediately, she got out of her chair, squared off to the boy, and passionately yelled, "Yes, it is, Matthew! I KNOW ALL ABOUT HUMAN NATURE!"

The head teacher yelled across the room for Sara to get back in her seat. Matthew and I just stared at each other, wide-eyed, wondering if we just heard what we thought we heard. I should have said something, but I couldn't even think of a response to that. I just looked at that little girl and let the truth of the conversation hit me: Women have it all figured out from a very young age. They know *all* about human nature.

YOU CAN'T JUDGE A BOOK BY ITS COVER

I can't count how many times I received dating advice from those kids that year. For some reason, they were always so shocked whenever I told them I was single. . . . If you ever need some motivation to start dating, just tell a kid you're not married and watch the expression of shock that covers their face. It could motivate the most hard-hearted of individuals to rethink their dating life.

As funny as those students were, it was still very apparent they were in that type of classroom for a reason. The littlest things would often trigger outburst and angry tantrums. Because they had so many struggles behaviorally, they needed constant supervision in the classroom as well as on the bus to and from school. Since it meant three more hours of paid work per day and a free ride to and from work, I agreed to be the bus aide, but I never expected it to be so hard.

I got up early each morning, rode the entire route on the bus, and then worked with those same kids all day long. At the end of each school day I'd board the bus again and watch the children leave the bus and walk to their homes. It was during those pickups and drop-offs that I saw that maybe a source of their behavior may have been due to their support—or lack thereof—at home. I saw what kinds of homes they came from, if they came to school clean or dirty, wearing new clothes or tattered clothes. I got an idea of how they lived even without walking inside their homes.

I saw how they started their school day each morning and how they ended their school day each afternoon. I was impressed by the long hours they spent at school and how hard they all tried to do their best, despite the "labels" they had gotten from other students or from their previous teachers. I saw enough to gain many glimpses into the hardships of their life and I sometimes felt like I spent more time with some of these kids than their parents did.

What I learned from riding that bus, getting a glimpse into the lives of those kids was this:

You can't judge anyone's determination or potential simply by how they look or based on their current circumstances.

This idea was expressed perfectly in *The Pursuit of Happyness* during the scene where Chris Gardner (Will Smith) shows up for a job interview in his grubbiest clothes because he ran all the way from the police station after being arrested on a parking ticket violation.

If you haven't seen it in a while, Chris is covered in paint, wearing old jeans and a tank top under his tattered jacket.

One man, Martin Frohm, asks, "What would you say if a man walked in here with no shirt, and I hired him? What would you say?"

Chris replies, "He must have had on some really nice pants."

Chris impressed the businessmen in that office with his determination, and he got the job despite his appearance.

> NEVER JUDGE SOMEONE BASED ON APPEARANCE. YOU DON'T KNOW WHAT THEY'VE GONE THROUGH JUST TO BE WHERE THEY ARE AT THAT MOMENT.

He didn't have much of a choice in what he wore that day due to his personal circumstances.[1] Even though I was the "teacher" those kids taught *me* that no matter where we come from, ultimately, our happiness comes down to whether we choose to be happy or not. Whether you come from very little or a lot, you can accomplish so much more than you thought you were capable of if you are determined to get there. I learned an inspiring example of this from a nine-year-old boy named Andres.

THE SECRET TO HAPPINESS

Andres moved into our classroom a few months into the school year because of his behavior at his other school. He tried to do his best in our class, but pretty soon, he'd returned to talking back and throwing fits. I approached the head teacher one day after one of his incidents and explained my frustration with Andres, finishing with, "He's a tough kid."

She listened to me and said, "Well, his family situation is even tougher. He actually lives in a one-bedroom apartment with a dozen other people."

As soon as I heard that, I was immediately humbled. It was almost like a physical slap to the face. The struggles these kids faced were suddenly so real to me that I wasn't sure how to even respond.

Thirteen people in a one-bedroom apartment meant Andres probably lived in constant chaos, no privacy or anything like that. And just like so many of the kids in that class, he would wake up each morning and have to get himself and his siblings ready for school. He had to get himself to the bus and take on an "adult" role even though he was still a little child.

These kids had struggles I could never imagine living with at their age. Suddenly I understood why they acted out, why they had days when they demanded attention or sulked or talked back.

I snapped back to reality. "These kids are real."

As I watched Andres the rest of that week and thought of his living situation, I realized that besides his tantrums, he was actually a pretty happy kid; he was always smiling and dancing around the classroom. I wanted to ask him how he stayed so happy all of the time.

When it was time for math the kids all separated into assigned groups and Andres came over to my table in the back of the classroom. I started them on their assignment and knew this was my chance to ask him.

Not wanting to get him off task, but really wanting to know his secret to happiness, I quietly said, "Hey, Andres, I noticed you're positive and happy all the time. . . . What do you do to be so happy in life?"

He thought about it a minute, looked up, leaned in, and asked quietly, "Do you want to know the secret?"

I started to get worried, hoping that his secret wasn't going to be something illegal that I would have to report him for.

I finally said, "Uh, yeah."

He leaned farther across the table, looked around as though to make sure no one else could hear, and said, "In the mornings . . . I wake up . . . and I *dance*."

Relief cascaded over me. Partly because I was glad what he did was legal, but mainly because of the simplicity of the life lesson he just taught me.

Of course, it wasn't what I expected either. "You dance?"

He shrugged a little. "Yeah. I dance."

"That's cool."

He said, "Yeah. In the mornings I just get up and turn on a little hip-hop music and I dance."

Then I thought of how crowded it would be with thirteen people in one apartment and I asked, "Doesn't that wake the other people up in your house?"

"Yeah," he said. "But it makes me happy so I do it anyway." He dropped his head back down toward his schoolwork and started in on his math again as if I'd never even asked him the question. A moment later, he quietly mumbled, "That's just what I do."

THE STUDENTS BECAME THE TEACHERS

DANCE MORE.
FROWN LESS.

This nine-year-old kid taught me that in order to be happy you have to find something you're passionate about and just do it. He wasn't even old enough to realize how important this lesson was. He just knew that dancing made him happy, so he danced . . . even if it meant waking up the people around him . . . he knew he had to take time for himself.

These kids took life one day at a time and they each found a way to be happy. I'm sure they had those days where they had to hit a reset button, just like that day when Andres threw his fits. But once you get beyond that, you just keep dancing. You find your happiness and you let it guide you through your day.

As with all my experiences in life, I'm still learning from my time at that elementary school. I constantly think back to the priceless lessons I was taught by those kids around that horseshoe table in the back of the classroom.

NOTE

1. Will Smith and James Karen, *The Pursuit of Happyness*, directed by Gabriele Muccino (Culver City, California: Columbia Pictures, 2006), DVD.

9

IT'S A DATE!

You remember Sara, right? She was my behavioral student who knew all about human nature? One time I told her about a date I was going on and I asked her if she had any advice. Without taking a second to think about it she said, "Dress up nice, take the girl out some place nice, then if you have a crush on her and she has a crush on you, marry her."

I think she may have oversimplified relationships a bit.

Since I am not married, I feel like I am not really qualified to give dating advice, because if I really knew what I was talking about . . . wouldn't I be married? Sometimes dating can be intimidating, just like life can be a bit scary. I have definitely had more than my fair share of awkward dating experiences and cold rejections. In fact, I remember one time I finally got up the courage to call a girl I'd had a few conversations with at school. After a few rings on the phone, I heard her answer and say, "Oh it's another boy. . . . It's okay . . . I totally don't like this guy."

In a somewhat confused voice, I said, "Hello?"

On the other end I heard her say, "Oh no!," shuffle around, and then hang up. She must have answered on accident and not known that I could hear what she was saying.

I texted her, "Haha, that was awkward. Have a great summer." Later she apologized, but I told her not to worry about it because I thought it was hilarious. Also, now I get to write about it in my book that will be published for the entire world to see, so I guess you all get the last laugh. Or maybe there will never be a last laugh. It's just too funny.

Regardless of my current relationship status, I feel like dating has added so much to my personality and I couldn't continue this book without sharing some of the dating experiences in my life and how they had an effect on my getting to where I am today. Hopefully what you read in this chapter will help you find joy in your dating journey, and learn to laugh at the rejections.

DATING IN PROVO

When I wasn't at school or work, I was thinking about dating. Scratch that. I thought about dating all the time. I want to have my own family someday, and in order to do that I need to date people, and in order to date people, I need to be social. The social/dating scene in Provo is an experience unlike any other. When speaking of dating, people often say "There are plenty of fish in the sea." But in Provo, dating is like taking all the fish in the sea and putting them inside a kiddie pool. The majority of people living in the city and going to school are members of The Church of Jesus Christ of Latter-day Saints. As members of the church, we believe in being chaste before marriage and in refraining from drugs or alcohol of any kind. That means there is never a shortage of fun, wholesome people you can ask out and go on fun, wholesome dates with. And by wholesome, I mean cheesy and slightly awkward.

Here is a list of just a few of the ones I've done.

- Go out for cupcakes and have a happy un-birthday party.

- Make a list of random items/situations you might find around town and try and get a picture with as many as possible in a short amount of time. This one is great for group dates.
- Write a song together and perform it at an open mic night.
- Make cookies together and go deliver them to a friend that may need a little pick-me-up.
- Go dancing. If there's no place to go, take your own music and dance in the park.
- Go to a bookstore and pick out children's books with titles that best describe you or your date. Then sit with your date and read them to each other.

Now, let me be first to say that not every date you go on with someone needs to be a super creative date that sounds like it came straight out of a television dating show. In fact, some of my favorite dates have been as simple as grabbing lunch for an hour and chatting about our lives. It's just good to have a few creative ones on hand when no other ideas come to mind because it really ruins a good date when you sit there for an hour going, "What do you want to do tonight?"

"I don't know. What do you want to do?"

"Whatever you want. I just want you to be happy."

"No, you decide."

Who knows, you might even use one of the ideas I listed and your date will be so impressed that when he/she asks how you came up with the idea for such a fun date, you'll say you read about it in Stuart Edge's book and he/she will tell you how much he/she loves Stuart Edge videos and had no idea that he had a book out and then you will talk all about it and he/she will be so impressed that he/she will fall in love with you in that very moment and confess his/her desire to spend the rest of his/her life with you. It's not very likely, but I'm just saying . . . it *could* happen.

DATING ADVENTURES

The moment I moved to Provo, I was anxious to start using some of my date ideas so I wasted no time in looking for a place I could go to put myself in a situation where I could meet the future Mrs. Edge. It was Saturday night and I'd heard there was a place downtown that had country dancing. I hadn't met anybody besides my roommates yet, so I went alone, thinking I could make some new friends and maybe even find someone to ask out on a date. I stepped onto the dance floor and my eye caught hold of beautiful girl in a green shirt being twirled around and lifted up by her partner. I assumed she was single because as soon as one song was done, she would immediately get asked by another guy to dance.

Sometime during the night I bumped into her on my way to the drinking fountain. I knew I probably only had two seconds to ask her to dance before someone else beat me to it, so I quickly put my need for water on hold, and asked her to dance. I had more fun dancing with her than I did with anyone else all night. And she was definitely as good of a dancer as she looked.

After our dance, she told me her name was Emily and asked me where I was from. I told her a bit about myself and that I had just moved to Provo and was living at an apartment complex called Raintree. Excitedly, she told me that was the same complex she lived in! Not only was it the same complex, but when I told her what building I was in, she said that was the building right next to hers, which meant we would be in the same church building on Sunday. We danced a few more times that night, invested in some small talk, and then I left, convinced I had just found my wife not even six hours into living in Provo.

When I got home that night, I told my roommates about Emily and they actually all knew her. "Emily's amazing," they said. "She's really smart, super strong in the church, and all the guys want to date her." I started to get a little nervous at the thought of having to compete with other guys for her attention. While I am confident in many areas of my life, I'm not the kind of guy who likes to fight for attention—I would definitely not be the alpha male in a pack of wolves. But I felt like we really got along and I really wanted to ask her out. Besides, how many of those other guys could dance as well as me?

I saw her at church the next day and thought of asking her out then, but for some reason, the energy I felt between us the night we danced wasn't there anymore, and I couldn't seem to carry a conversation with her. It was just really awkward and I didn't know how to handle it. I saw her a few more times at activities during the week, but no matter how much I rehearsed the conversation in my head, every time I tried to talk to her, I forgot what I wanted to say. It's moments like that I wish I could yell out "LINE PLEASE!" and someone would call out to me the next thing I should say. Instead, I fumbled on my words and talked about the most generic things like school and work, until other guys swooped in and started sweet-talking their way into the conversation.

A DATE I WILL *NEVER* FORGET

One day, with a little pep talk from my roommates, I finally got the courage to ask her out. I walked over to her apartment and in front of all her roommates, asked her on a date for later that week. She agreed to go, although her enthusiasm about it didn't match the reaction I envisioned in my mind.

Regardless, I was excited that she said yes and I was finally going out on a date. I was still worried I might not know what to say around her, so I planned out this extravagant game to go along with miniature golf. I called it "Get-to-Know-You Golf." I printed some questions on slips of paper that would be great for getting to know someone. The questions were rated according to score, so the better we scored on each hole, the easier the question we each had to answer got. And if you got a hole in one, the other person had to do something crazy.

My little gimmick didn't work. It just made the date even more awkward. We were the only ones on the mini golf course, and after a few holes, the only time we spoke to each other was when we were pulling questions from the bag. I snuck in a few questions about dancing the moonwalk, so I could show off my moonwalking skills to her, but I quickly learned it's nearly impossible to moonwalk on artificial turf with tennis shoes. I think we were both relieved when the game was over. We each just wanted to get home and be done with the date. But then I suggested ice cream.

She said, "Sure. Why not? There's a place near our apartment we can go to."

Going to a place packed with people and a football game on the television behind us helped our interaction. We had distractions to stimulate our conversation, but it wasn't enough to keep it going. After another moment of silence, I realized I better do something to keep a conversation going. I noticed she had something on her chin, so I pointed and said, "You've got ice cream right there."

She swiped at it but missed.

I motioned toward her chin again, trying to be flirty.

The second time she swiped, we both realized that it wasn't ice cream at all but a zit.

(Aaaaand this is why I'm still single.)

We both looked away, pretending to watch the football game, the silence between us nearly driving me crazy. I wanted to jump up on the table like some kind of hero-gentleman, sending our ice cream crashing to the ground to declare my love for her. I wanted to grab her hand and tell her the zit didn't matter because she was still beautiful to me . . . and follow that up with a proposal.

That's what happened inside my head. But my mouth simply asked, "Do you want to stay and finish watching the game?"

The game had just entered overtime, and we were both pretty into it, so I was sure we could just go back to that common interest. But instead she just said "No, I'm good."

As we walked out to the car, I thought, maybe she didn't know she had a zit, and it was just all in my head. I opened the door on her side of the car, and then walked around the back to my side. As I walked around, I looked through the back window and saw her pull down the visor mirror and frantically check her face.

The drive back to our apartment complex was about sixty seconds long, but it felt like sixty minutes. I said a lot of charming things to her in my mind on the way back, but we didn't speak to each other once. I dropped her off and sulkily walked back to my apartment. I felt so bad. What if this girl was my one true love, and I just blew it because of a stupid golf game and some ice cream?

For some motivation the next day I Googled stories of people that still got married despite having horrible first dates. While it did give me some good laughs and helped me look at the situation a little more lightheartedly, it didn't change much with my relationship with Emily. While we never went out on another date again, we did become casual friends seeing each other here and there at church activities. However, to this day we have never addressed the zit-uation. . . .

Maybe someday, if I have my own talk show, I will invite her onto the show and get her side of the story.

THE PEOPLE WE MEET CAN PREPARE US FOR THE FUTURE

I quickly learned in life that dating is not as easy as Sara made it out to be. While dating hasn't always gone as planned, I have met some amazing people in my life because of it, and have been inspired to better myself. Sometimes heartbreaks lead us to bigger and better things. As they say, "When one door closes, another door opens."

One relationship like that in particular was with a girl named Katie. I met Katie in the spring of 2011, just a few weeks before the end of the school year. She was so fun. We just clicked. We talked easily and she had a great sense of humor. We saw each other every day, and it just felt right.

My time working at the elementary school was coming down to its final days and I already had a summer job lined up selling pest control. The job, however, was all the way in Philadelphia, and as I began spending more time with Katie, the thought of leaving for the entire summer did not sound appealing. What if it ruined this friendship I was building with her?

After a lot of thought, I called the pest control company and told them I decided I would not be working for them this summer. They were not too happy about that, considering I was supposed to be out there in just a few days, but I felt at peace with the decision I'd made, and knew that it was the right thing for me at the time.

I ran over to Katie's apartment and told her the news that I was now going to be able to spend the entire summer with her and we could continue getting to know each other. She gave me a big hug and expressed her excitement too, but then asked, "What are you going to do for a job?"

Oh crap . . . I thought. My contract at the school was ending in three days. They asked me if I wanted to extend into summer school, but since I had been planning on doing summer sales, I had declined and now all the positions were filled. I needed to find a job and fast.

A CRAPPY JOB

Maybe it was because my first thought was "Oh crap," but not long after that, I remembered my Aunt Diane telling me about a guy in her neighborhood that owned a porta-potty business and was looking for some extra workers. She actually told me about the job nine months earlier when I first moved to Provo, but I declined the invitation because number one, I already had the school job lined up. And number two, cleaning porta-potties? Enough said.

At this point, however, I no longer cared what I did for work, as long as it was paid, and I could start as soon as possible. I called up Greg, who owned the business, and left a voice mail saying I was interested in a job cleaning porta-potties. (I never imagined I'd ever leave a voice mail like that at any point in my life.) A few days later he called me back and said he just had a guy put in his two weeks' notice, so they could start training me in one week. Wow. I now had the entire summer to spend building my relationship with Katie, and I had a job. Life seemed perfect. I couldn't believe it had all happened so fast. Only a few days before that, I was planning on selling pest control in Philadelphia, and now I'd be cleaning porta-potties in Provo.

CHANGE OF PLANS

If you have learned anything about my life while reading this book, though, it's that when something is going well, usually it means something difficult is right around the corner. And it's no different in this case, because one morning, a few days after I told Katie I was staying, she came to my apartment to tell me we should stop seeing each other. The conversation was pretty quick and straightforward and she didn't stay long. After she left I sunk into the giant beanbag in my apartment, thinking about how the girl I quit my job for didn't want to see me now. What made it worse was when I realized that it was only a few hours until I would start my new job cleaning porta-potties. It's safe to say that was the crappiest day of my life.

THE PORTA-POTTY BUSINESS IS NOT SOMETHING YOU WANT TO FALL INTO.

10

HOW MY CRAPPY JOB CHANGED MY LIFE

So, there I was, twenty-two, single, and reeking of porta-potties. That first day on the job was so hard. The only reason I took the job was because it meant I would get to be close to a girl, and now that she was out of the picture, I had no desire to work there.

I'm sure there are many of you out there that have some questions about the portable restroom business, so let me explain a little.

First of all, yes, you do get used to the smell. Not sure if that's a good thing or a bad thing. I'll let you decide.

It takes about three to five minutes to service a porta-potty. Unless it was tipped over on the door side . . . then it takes fifteen minutes. Toilets are generally serviced once a week.

On a normal day, I woke up at 4:30 a.m., arrived at work by 5 a.m., printed all the papers for my route, and was on the road cleaning my first toilet of the day by 5:30 a.m. I wore long pants, boots, gloves, and a heavy work coat. In the winter it was great because I was bundled up, but in the summer it was hot and uncomfortable and since I was the youngest employee, they gave me the truck without any air-conditioning. My main route was a big freeway project in Utah where I'd clean seventy-five to a hundred porta-potties per day. It was not uncommon for me to work twelve to fifteen hours each day during the summer months. If I wasn't servicing toilets on the freeway or home construction sites, I was helping set up a hundred to two hundred porta-potties for fairs and rodeos. I always hated doing those because people always gave me the weirdest looks as they pointed and laughed at me. I used to get really embarrassed. But after a while I got over it and didn't really care anymore.

If dating wasn't already hard enough with a "normal" job, cleaning toilets didn't make it any easier. Now, you may not believe this, but being a portable restroom cleaner isn't the most glamorous job in the world. But it was paying my bills. Even at that, it wasn't something to brag about to a girl you had just met.

I would meet great girls at all types of events, but the moment I told them what I did for work, and they realized I wasn't joking, they stopped showing interest and I never heard from them again.

I started to refer to my job title as "Sanitation Engineer" or "Biohazard Waste Disposal Specialist." It helped a little, but eventually people saw right through the pompous name.

However, it was job, and I was grateful to have it. So, day after day, I drove all around Utah cleaning toilets in the hot summer air . . . alone.

STUCK IN A CRAPPY SITUATION

As crappy as the job was, there were some benefits. It paid very well . . . nearly four or five dollars an hour *more* than most of my friends were making, and when it came time for fall semester at UVU, they were flexible with my class schedule. For a while, I was able to balance school, work, and a social life. However, in the middle of the year, ownership of the company changed and they started requiring more time of me, which made it harder to work around school. I had to give so much attention to my job that I started to neglect important things like the social, educational, and spiritual parts of my life. During the spring semester I had to drop all but two of my classes, just so I could stay afloat. I barely survived that semester and was left examining my life, wondering what in the world I was doing. I was now a year into cleaning porta-potties and I wondered why I hadn't quit my job already. I wanted so badly to quit my job and find work somewhere else. I didn't care how little it paid, as long as I didn't have to clean another toilet. However, I couldn't just quit my job, because earlier that year I had accidentally backed into a garage door, causing nearly a thousand dollars in damages. Because it was my fault, I was responsible to reimburse the company to repair the door. I could either pay for it out of my own pocket or be incident-free for a full year and they would waive the fee. The only problem was that even though I had worked so hard over the past year at a pretty decent hourly wage, somehow I had nothing left in my bank account. Where had it all gone? All that work, all that sweat, all that humiliation, and I had nothing to show for it.

On top of that, school was a constant struggle and I still had no idea what I wanted to do for a career. Girls didn't want to date me, and since I was always so exhausted after work, all I could do was go home and sleep, eliminating any chance for a social life. My life had reached a tipping point and I was not looking forward to another summer cleaning porta-potties in an un-air-conditioned porta-prison, so I started developing my escape plan. Amidst all the crap I was dealing with, I had the smallest feeling I should not quit, and not make any changes to my situation, but I pushed the thought aside because I was tired of waiting and wanted to get a fresh start on things as quickly as possible.

Despite that feeling, my strategy was to finish my route that week and then tell the company I quit and they could use my last paycheck to pay for the damaged door. In the meantime, I'd find ways to save some money by moving to a cheaper apartment while I began my search for another job.

A CHANGE OF SCENERY

Right away, I sprung into action. I drove to an apartment in Provo that, during the summer, dropped their rent to only sixty dollars per month. I was paying two hundred and fifty dollars at my current place so I would instantly be saving a bunch of money. I signed the application without hesitation and handed it the lady in the main office. She asked to see my ID card and I realized I'd forgotten it at home. I rushed home as quickly as I could, and returned with everything I thought I'd need. For the second time, I handed over my signed application, this time accompanied by my identification. I was minutes away from being in a new apartment, when she asked for my deposit. I quickly realized I had forgotten my credit card in my rush. She informed me she couldn't accept my application until I had my deposit on hand and since it was getting late I'd have to bring it in the morning.

I returned back to my old apartment, tired, heart heavy, and knowing the feeling I'd had earlier about not changing my circumstances was real and I wasn't supposed to move from my current place. That was a hard thing to accept because I desperately wanted something different.

MAKING DEALS WITH GOD

I ripped up my application and fell to my knees and cried. I clasped my hands and began vocally crying to God. "Fine! I get it! I'm not supposed to move and I won't quit my job.

But how do you expect me to get anywhere in life if I'm stuck cleaning porta-potties?"

I was so upset. I could feel, though, that God was listening very closely to everything I had to say. As much as I wanted to deny it, the feeling I had was confirmed that the best thing for me to do was continue at my current job and not move out of my apartment. As I prayed, I decided to do something I had only tried one other time before, and it was to make a deal with God. Again, praying out loud, I said, "Okay, I won't quit my job and I won't move out, but I need to know what I should do for the rest of my life, I need to get a better job, and I need to get married."

I ended my prayer a few moments later, fully expecting to receive three phone calls. One from someone giving golden career advice, another from someone offering a job that paid fifty dollars an hour, and the last call from the girl of my dreams telling me she wanted to get married. Unfortunately my phone didn't ring once that night, and to this day I still haven't received that last phone call. But who knows, maybe she just lost my number.

The next day, I woke up at 4:30 a.m. and suited up to go clean porta-potties. As much as I wanted it to be different, I trusted that I was right where I needed to be at that time. I trusted God had some kind of plan in store for me, but I still wondered what good could possibly come from paying a higher rent and working a crappy job.

DON'T GET DISCOURAGED WHEN THINGS FALL THROUGH. IT USUALLY MEANS THERE'S SOMETHING BETTER JUST AROUND THE CORNER.

A NEW PERSPECTIVE

For the next three summer months, I continued my fifteen-hour workdays among the toilets. Not long after my prayer where I made a deal with God, I was prompted to find ways to make my fifteen hours more uplifting. In the past I had listened to talk radio in the truck because it made me feel like I wasn't alone, but I had grown tired of the negativity. So I decided to download thousands of inspirational and motivational talks to my phone and listen to them while I was working. A lot of these talks were formal, fifteen minute gospel-centered discourses given by leaders of the LDS Church, while others were hour-long informal and motivational interviews with people who had learned to live a Christ-centered life despite the challenges life had thrown at them.

Almost immediately after I began listening to those talks, I felt refreshed and I actually looked forward to work. It was like a breath of fresh air, and believe me, you need that every once in awhile when you're cleaning porta-potties every day.

LOOK FOR A WAY TO FILL THE DEAD-SPACE IN YOUR DAY WITH POSITIVE STORIES OR MUSIC.

All those talks put life back into perspective for me. It was encouraging to hear examples of other people who had gone through similar things that I was going through and to hear what they did to overcome their challenges, how they came to choose their careers, how they met their spouses, and so on. While I didn't have an answer yet to what I should do, I felt like I had started to reconnect with the things that came naturally to me and I remembered the excitement I got as a child when

I would do things like performing and entertaining. All of that time driving from one porta-potty site to another allowed me the time I needed to begin thinking more clearly about what some of my strengths were and what I could contribute to the world. I actually loved the inspiration I was feeling so much that I started looking forward to finding tipped-over porta-potties because it meant an extra fifteen minutes of work where I could listen to one more talk that day.

Two talks in particular changed my outlook on life and were the answer to one of my questions. I remember the day I listened to these talks like it was yesterday. I had been working on the giant freeway project and, since they were getting close to finishing construction, I was four hours ahead of schedule because there were only half as many toilets to clean. Near the end of my day I listened a man named Gary Ceran tell his story.

WILLING TO FORGIVE

Gary Ceran lost his wife and two of his children when their car was hit by a drunk driver on Christmas Eve in 2006. As he surveyed the scene of the accident, his car smashed, his loved ones in body bags, and Christmas packages scattered across the road, Gary felt "an utter sense of disparage and hopelessness."

But as Gary was loaded into the ambulance, he knew there was only one way he could move on. He had to forgive the intoxicated driver and take care of his surviving children.[1]

His story inspired people around the world when it happened in 2006 and it inspired me that day in 2012 as I sat in my filthy work clothes on a construction site in my porta-potty truck.

MY TURNING POINT

As I listened to Gary's talk, I was inspired by his willingness to forgive. I don't know what it was, but something about Gary's story hit me, and I immediately knew the answer to what I wanted to do the rest of my life. The answer came to my mind so clearly. "I want to tell people's stories and I want to inspire other people with those stories."

As those thoughts coursed through my mind, I distinctly had the impression that I should do just that, tell people's stories. I replayed that

> SOMETIMES INSPIRATION STRIKES US WHERE/WHEN WE LEAST EXPECT IT. IT'S SO FUNNY TO ME THAT SUCH A POWERFUL AND LIFE-CHANGING THOUGHT CAME TO ME WHILE I WAS CLEANING A TOILET.

talk two or three times, the same impression coming to me over and over. *Tell people's stories and inspire people with those stories.*

That talk was quite literally my turning point. I was so excited because I finally had some direction in life. However, I began to wonder *how* I was going to tell people's stories? Through what means? A post on Facebook? Writing an article in a local magazine? Shouting it from the top of a porta-potty? It is not coincidence that the very next talk following Gary Ceran's was about a German filmmaker named Peter Czerny.

FOLLOWING A DREAM

Peter Czerny was born in Germany during World War II. His father was drafted into the German army, leaving his mother to tend to their children. Though he was young at the time, just four years old, he still remembers being evacuated from his home and moved into their first refugee camp while his father was away fighting. Reunited with his father at five years old, his family made their away across Germany, eventually immigrating to the United States when Peter was twelve.

Even though he didn't speak a word of English, he started school immediately because he had a dream to fulfill. He wanted, more than anything, to be a filmmaker. Even when there was no way for Peter to even own a camera, he made filmstrips from paper and told the stories he'd one day film.

He ended up getting a job with The Church of Jesus Christ of Latter-day Saints, filming and editing their Mormon Messages.

INSPIRATION STRIKES

When he started talking about his desire to be a filmmaker, everything clicked for me. I pulled my truck over and just sat there. My mind was going a million miles an hour connecting all the dots of everything that had happened to me up to that point and how everything was connected in some way. Had I quit my job a few months ago, I might not have had this moment to listen to these talks which would then help answer some of the things I was wondering most about.

I felt like I finally found a purpose and something to work toward. I was going tell people's stories through video. The only problem was that meant I would need to take back the promise I made to myself as a young teen in Mexico, when I swore I would never make videos for a living.

NOTE

1. Pat Reavy, "'Letting Go of Poison': In Wake of Grief, Families Offer Astonishing Acts of Forgiveness," *Deseret News*, September 4, 2011.

11

THE PIECES START COMING TOGETHER

I t hadn't taken long for me to see why it was so important for me to keep my job cleaning porta-potties. It had to do with being in the right place at the right time and in the right circumstance to hear the right message.

By staying at my porta-potty job, I started listening to the talks that held the answer to a career path I should embark on. I didn't know exactly where to start, but I figured if I wanted to start making videos, I would need some equipment. Probably a camera.

I went home that night and did some research about which camera I should buy. I only had a few hundred dollars saved up but I used it all to buy my very first camera. It was a Canon T4i and when it arrived a few days later, I started videoing everything I could think of. I took that camera everywhere: dances, parties, you name it. I even took it on a date once. (I used it as a way to get out of talking about my current

> **MOST CELL PHONES HAVE GREAT VIDEO CAMERAS NOW. DON'T BE AFRAID TO USE ONE FOR YOUR FIRST VIDEOS.**

job situation.) I quickly learned that holding a camera is like a magnet for attention and an easy conversation starter.

THE CAMPOUT

Remember, though, how I also felt like I was supposed to stay in my current apartment? I'd experienced the rewards of sticking with my job, but, up to this point, nothing exciting had happened because of not moving into a less expensive apartment. Actually, our complex *did* throw a pool party once with free hot dogs and hamburgers, but I really hoped the reason for my staying wasn't so I could get a sunburn and stuff my face with free food. I later found out it was so I could have run into the *one* person in my current apartment complex who could get me my first job making YouTube videos.

Toward the end of the summer, our complex was having an overnight camping trip up in the mountains. I didn't think I'd be able to go because I would most likely have my head in a porta-potty somewhere. But on the day of the campout I got done with my route in record time, which gave me just enough time to change, pack, and meet the group at the apartment clubhouse just before they carpooled up to the mountain.

During the campout, a guy from the complex named Tyler approached me and started making small talk about my camera, which I obviously had with me. I'd had that camera for almost a month and took it everywhere. I almost made a video about cleaning a porta-potty once. I later decided I would do mankind a favor and *not* show what that process was like.

"You make videos?" he asked.

"I don't really yet, but I would like to," I told him.

"I can probably get you an internship making YouTube videos if you'd like," he said.

He now had my full attention.

CHAPTER 11

"The company I work for, Orabrush, needs some help making YouTube videos for their channel," he explained.

I had no idea what an Orabrush was, but I'd been praying for the opportunity to find a job making videos, so I was willing to take whatever came my way. We talked a little more about the job and other video-making adventures for the remainder of the outing.

The next day he called me to confirm that I could come in and help on one of their shoots. I was ecstatic. It was almost too easy. Everything seemed to just be falling in my lap. It then hit me that had I signed the contract for the cheaper apartment, I would not have gone on the campout for the complex I was currently living in, which meant I would not have met Tyler, and I would not have found a job making videos. I felt so blessed that my questions were being answered, one by one.

FLUSHING MY PORTA-POTTY JOB

The first day I walked into Orabrush, I knew it was the place for me. I could almost see the creative energy flowing through the office. I was introduced to the team and learned that Orabrush was a company that made fun, viral YouTube videos to promote their product . . . a tongue cleaner that I helped prevent bad breath. My first responsibility was sanding down two acrylic rods to look like toothbrush bristles, and then helped run sound for the video shoot that followed. I felt right at home, and immediately knew I wanted to work there for a very long time.

I left the office that day and called my manager at the porta-potty job. I was nervous what he would say, because when ownership changed, the company got a bit stricter.

"I need to quit," I said.

He said, "You've got about six months left before you can quit this job or you owe a thousand dollars for that garage door you backed into."

I hadn't worked long enough to pay it back and I didn't have enough money to cover the damage outright, but I would sacrifice anything to finally get out of that job. "I'd like to pay the fee and quit," I said. "I have another job lined up that I don't want to lose."

Even though there were only three weeks left on the freeway project, it would be very difficult for them to find guys that could get the route done. I knew I was valuable to them right now, so I was hoping we could make some kind of a deal.

There was a long pause on the line and then he said, "Finish out your three weeks and I'll waive your fee. That way I won't have to train anyone else or figure out a way to get someone to cover your route once you're gone."

I breathed a sigh of relief knowing I could get out of my job, but it was frustrating to think I still had to endure another three weeks as a Biohazard Waste Disposal Specialist when my new career in video making was finally within reach.

Three weeks went by and on August 12, 2012, I cleaned my last porta-potty. Oddly, I had mixed feelings. I'm not going to say I shed a tear over it, but knowing I would never clean another porta-potty caused me to reflect on how grateful I was for the chance to do something so unique. While I was happy to be done with that job and able to focus solely on making videos, I thought about how much those porta-potties had changed me. (Not to mention how I had painstakingly changed them.) Week after week, I scrubbed, sanitized, and repaired those little outhouses; but in a strange way, cleaning those porta-potties had cleansed me as well. It was the filthiest, yet most spiritual job I had ever had. I learned so much about who I was, and the things I wanted to do to help inspire the world.

That crappy job really did change my life.

PART 3
VIRAL VIDEOS

A YouTube meeting with some of the most popular YouTubers in Utah. At the time this picture was taken, I had nine subscribers.

12

REIMAGINING THE MISTLETOE TRADITION

So there I was, twenty-three years old, still single, but no longer smelling of porta-potties.

I loved what I was learning at Orabrush, and the passion of filmmaking I had felt as young teenager in Mexico was coming back to me. I began to see I had a natural ability for creating videos.

My boss, Jeffrey, actually encouraged my creative ideas and even said he'd be disappointed in me if I didn't pursue my own video ventures. I was so confused, even a little offended, at his interest in my life outside of work. But I later realized that he had just given me the golden career advice I had been praying for. Even though I was helping to make YouTube videos for Orabrush, I began making a few of my own videos in my spare time. However, I still didn't know anything about how to make a video successful on the web. Little did I know that in just a few days, I was about to experience a viral video unlike ever before.

THURSDAY, DECEMBER 6, 2012

I was finishing up an edit for an Orabrush video when some coworkers came up to me and asked if I was going to

Devin Supertramp's presentation on how to be successful on YouTube. I loved watching Devin's videos and was excited to hear his secrets on how to make fun, viral videos.

We got to Devin's house, and it was packed. As I walked around and mingled, people asked me what kind of YouTube channel I had. I was caught off guard by what seemed to me to be a trivial question. Why would anyone want to know what *kind* of YouTube channel I had? I just used YouTube to upload random music videos or skits I filmed with friends. I admitted that I didn't really have one, and was just part of the Orabrush crew. As I got to know more of the attendees, I learned that many of them had themed content for their YouTube channels. I talked to one guy who only posted parkour videos, while another girl I met only posted beauty vlogs. I realized, then, that these people were using YouTube in a way I had never even thought of before. They were using it to build an audience for their videos, and since the Internet reached all across the world, they had the potential to be seen by millions.

During Devin's presentation, I learned that it was even possible to earn money making YouTube videos! Everything I had heard that night gave me this feeling like I could do anything I set my mind to. To end his presentation, Devin said, "Last year, Lindsey Stirling attended a meeting like this and now she's got a growing YouTube channel. Who knows, maybe someone attending tonight will make it big by next year."

As soon as he spoke those words, I told myself, *That's going to be me. I'm going to be the one who makes it big.*

After the presentation, I spoke with some of the successful YouTubers about my plans to start a successful channel and asked if they'd mind sharing one of the few videos I had made so far.

I could tell some of them were just being nice when they said, "Sure" or "Maybe." Others kind of dismissed me and that was the end of it. Still, I listened to everything they had to say that night, and I felt like I could make it too. I felt like all I needed was to come up with the right idea and I'd be getting views just like everyone else at the party. I left for home determined to not sleep until I had come up with my first big video idea.

> DON'T GIVE UP ON YOUR IDEAS. PURSUE THEM AND OWN THEM.

SATURDAY, DECEMBER 8, 2012

We met at Devin's house on a Thursday. Saturday night, I attended a Christmas party with my friend Nate. There must have been something in the eggnog, because I was seeing ideas for videos everywhere I looked. I never thought an awkward Christmas party could be more inspiring than any amount of brainstorming or planning.

Nate and I noticed a mistletoe at the party, but everybody was avoiding it like it was an angry wasp's nest. Nobody was kissing. It actually created a strange tension around the mistletoe, almost like this vibe warning people not to enter that "zone."

"Do you think anyone actually kisses under mistletoe anymore?" I asked.

"Not at this party," Nate said. "It's actually a little awkward."

I considered that for a minute, the awkwardness of the situation could be funny if we captured it the right way.

"Do you think this would make for a funny video?" I finally asked.

This is a picture taken at the Christmas party I went to. If you look closely, you can see the mistletoe hanging in the doorway!

Nate and I joked about how we could use the mistletoe in a video and we came up with a comedy skit about a guy who was trying to get girls to stand under the mistletoe with him by asking ridiculous questions.

It could be really funny, but was it enough to be a hit?

All throughout church on Sunday I had new ideas rolling around in my head. Finally I asked Nate, "What if we did it for real? If it wasn't a skit, but real people asking strangers their opinion of the mistletoe tradition and then a real mistletoe falls from the ceiling?"

It took quite a bit of talking to get Nate

> **IF YOU'RE NOT SURE YOUR IDEAS ARE POWERFUL ENOUGH, THINK ABOUT EVERY POSSIBLE ANGLE. DETERMINE THE BEST WAY TO GET THE OUTCOME YOU'RE HOPING FOR AND FIND A WAY TO MAKE IT HAPPEN.**

to kiss strangers under the mistletoe. But it didn't take much time to set it up. We planned to meet up Monday afternoon at the Wilkinson Center on Brigham Young University's campus with some borrowed film equipment.

MONDAY, DECEMBER 10, 2012

The Wilkinson Center is the student center for anyone attending BYU. It's the place to go bowling or to play pool or ping-pong. There's a food court on the main floor so it attracts a lot of people, all the time. What caught my eye was the main floor close to the food court, known as the terrace. The floor above the terrace opens up so that a balcony overlooks it. The balcony would be the perfect place to drop the mistletoe from without being noticed.

We got everyone in their places and waited for people to walk by. Holding clipboards so we looked official, we stopped them, asked them some false survey questions about Christmas traditions, and then, like a dove descending from the heavens, the mistletoe dropped on cue, resting in the air ever so gently above the head of the interviewer.

There were smiles all around. Students began to call their friends over to watch the prank from afar. I felt like we had something good on our hands. After an hour and a half of lip locks with strangers, and even one giant slap on the face (poor Nate), we went to Orabrush to edit the video.

As I looked through the footage from that night, I still felt like something was missing. I didn't know what it was, it just felt like we needed more reactions. All my friends called me crazy, but I insisted we go back again the next day.

TUESDAY, DECEMBER 11, 2012

At work I told my friend Kaitlin about the video we had filmed the night before and that we were going back again to get more reactions. She thought it was a funny idea and said she would love to help. I was so glad I made the push to go back a second day because having a girl interviewer added an entirely new dynamic to the video.

We finished filming the "Mistletoe Kissing Prank" at 8:30 that night and, again, I went straight to Orabrush to start editing. I downloaded my footage and started moving clips around; however, I felt like I wasn't getting anywhere with it. I was stuck. All I could do was simply stare at the screen. It was cool stuff, but how could I possibly condense it into a single video?

I ground my teeth together and thought of food and sleep. Maybe I should have taken time to eat, but no, I just had to get this put together. I felt this drive to make it happen but then my mind went completely blank. I had no idea how to edit a video like this. I was about to go home and give up on it . . . maybe I would work on it again in a few days . . . maybe a few weeks or . . . maybe never.

> **SOMETIMES YOU GET INTO A SLUMP AND YOU'VE JUST GOT TO PUSH THROUGH IT. THEN THINGS WILL START ROLLING.**

I'm not sure how long I stared at that footage, but I knew staring alone wouldn't get it edited. It was time to ask someone who always knew how to help.

I bowed my head and said a little prayer asking for direction. I just wanted to make something fun that people could watch to forget about their worries for a small moment.

Shortly afterward I felt inspired to take it one step at a time and start selecting my favorite clips from the overall video. I looked at the footage, picking out my favorite reactions, and dropping them into my time line. I did this over and over, clipping and editing until the video finally started to take shape.

This went on all night.

I got so zoned in that I completely lost track of time and people started showing up for our 9 a.m. production meeting. They stopped by my desk and checked out the video I was working on.

From the looks on their faces, I assumed they were impressed by something. Whether it was the fact that I hadn't slept all night or that my video was actually entertaining, I wasn't sure, until my friend Austin said, "I don't want to get your hopes up, but I wouldn't be surprised if this got a million views." A million views? Oh, that definitely got my hopes up.

TRYING TO FOCUS

Then my boss, Jeff, arrived and explained nicely that when you work an hourly job for someone else, it's good practice to actually work on *their* ideas each hour you're being paid.

So I turned my attention to my work at Orabrush, only my heart wasn't in it. I kept thinking of my mistletoe video, sitting alone on the computer, just waiting to be polished and posted.

> WHEREVER YOU ARE, BE ALL THERE.
>
> —JIM ELLIOT
>
> BASICALLY, IF YOU'RE AT WORK, BE AT WORK.

I kept trying to ignore the urge to work on my own video, but every now and then I'd pull it up, make a few adjustments and then switch back over to my Orabrush work.

It was painful. I was just waiting for everyone to leave so I could get back to my video.

When everyone left work, I pulled up the "Mistletoe Kissing Prank," no longer watching my time on a clock, and by midnight, I had a good enough cut that I uploaded it, shared it with some friends on Facebook and went home to get some rest.

The "Mistletoe Kissing Prank," was now on YouTube.

Getting interviewed by a local news station the day the mistletoe video went viral.

13

12/12/12

I woke up the next morning anxious to see how my video was doing. I looked at the view count and there were about sixty-six views. I thought to myself, *That makes sense. I think I have about sixty-six friends that might have seen it overnight.* But within a couple of minutes, I saw the view count increase to 301 views. *This doesn't make sense. I don't have three hundred friends.* Even though my heart was racing about the views on my video, back in the real world, I was running late for a meeting with a lawyer in Salt Lake about a video he hired me to edit. I was really excited because it was the first client I had booked on my own and I was starting to feel like a real businessman.

As I sat in the lawyer's office talking about the interview video he wanted to make, I really just wanted to be checking my phone. It's a good thing there wasn't any service in the building, otherwise I would have been very distracted, because little did I know that during that meeting, my mistletoe video was going viral and tens of thousands of people were learning my name. I continued going about my day like it was any other, trying to get a little extra work to keep some money coming in.

The meeting with the lawyer went a little long, which made me nervous because I had to get back to Orabrush for an important company meeting. As soon as I left the building, my phone connected to service again and began to chime with notifications. Was everyone at Orabrush

> SOMETIMES THINGS JUST HAPPEN WHEN YOU'RE NOT PAYING ATTENTION—AND IT'S BETTER THAT WAY.

letting me know I was late for the meeting? I checked a few of the messages and saw that it was just some friends and family telling me how much they liked the video. I checked the view count again and saw that it was still frozen at 301, but there were close to a hundred comments from peoples' names I didn't recognize. It was apparent that more than just a few of my friends had been watching the video.

All the way home from Salt Lake City, texts continued to come in from my friends and family. I had missed calls and a few messages that I couldn't check while driving. I knew, however, that some of them had to do with my video, and I was actually nervous to see what all the talk was about. My hands tightened on the steering wheel as I passed a semitruck. Was I in trouble? Was there something wrong with my video? Was I going to be fired from Orabrush for being late to the meeting?

> AS EXCITING AS HAVING A VIRAL VIDEO CAN BE, IT ALSO COMES WITH A TREMENDOUS AMOUNT OF PRESSURE.

I whipped into the Orabrush office parking lot and ran inside. I was already thirty minutes late to the meeting and was completely prepared to be fired as soon as I entered the building. As I walked into the office I was greeted with applause and pats on the back. *This is a strange way to fire someone.* A few of my coworkers were all gathered around a computer watching my video and they showed me all the websites that were sharing it. I didn't know the exact amount of views it was getting because back then YouTube's view count would stay frozen at 301 views for the first twenty-four hours. All I could judge the success of the video by at that time was the number of likes and comments it was getting. When my boss, Jeffrey, told me he's never seen a video go this big before, I got my hopes up.

Throughout the day I tried to get some work done at Orabrush, but I was constantly interrupted with emails requesting phone interviews. We even had a news crew come by and interview me. I've got to give a huge shout out to my boss, Jeffrey, and the team at Orabrush for the way they handled everything that day. They allowed me to take my calls, answer my emails, and do that interview right there at work. I'm so grateful for the support they showed me and for making me feel like the things I did outside of work were valued and appreciated.

That day was so surreal. There's really no other way to describe what I was feeling.

I hadn't ever really experienced it before, but the joy and excitement of that day were completely overwhelming—it was just too much joy, too much recognition in a short amount of time. I also experienced something else for the first time that day: the crash that comes after.

WHAT DO YOU DO WHEN YOUR VIDEO GOES VIRAL?

At the end of the day, when the view count finally was displayed, I saw it had one million views. I couldn't even fathom the number. Before, the idea of having a million people see my work was just that: an idea. Even more mind-blowing for me was the number of YouTube subscribers I started to get. Before posting the mistletoe video, I had a whopping total of nine subscribers to my YouTube channel. I'm pretty sure five of them were my own family. Planning to continue making videos though not having any idea what videos I would make or how I would make them, at the end of the video, I had invited people to subscribe to my channel. Apparently a lot of people wanted to see more videos, because by the end of the night I had more than twenty thousand new subscribers.

Late that night, as I watched the views continue to rise and thought about how many people were now following me, I began to panic. The feelings of anxiety that I had felt as a young boy began to rise inside me. A cold sweat came over me as my mind raced through all of the possible negative outcomes from so many people viewing my video. Nothing but good things were being said about the video so far, but what if tomorrow people started getting angry about it? What if people were offended and took it the wrong way? What if people got really mean in the YouTube comments? Would I be able to handle that?

I did the only thing I could think of and I called my mom.

"Pray for me," I told her. "I think my video just went viral."

"Isn't that a good thing?" she asked.

"No, Mom. That means more people are going to see it now."

She wasn't an expert when it came to YouTube videos, but she still must have been really confused, because why would anyone not want their video seen by millions of people?

I explained to her my anxieties about it, and she gave me the counsel she always gave me. "Just pray and you will be able to handle whatever comes your way."

Those words of counsel didn't rid me of the anxiety I was feeling, but they did help focus my nerves on things that actually mattered and that would help me make the most out of this situation.

IT WAS HARDER THAN I THOUGHT

By the end of the week, the "Mistletoe Kissing Prank" had been seen over ten million times. It had been shared by nearly every news/entertainment website and on countless news stations across the globe. People were even creating their own versions and putting them on YouTube.

Eventually everything slowed down and I got back to working on my Orabrush projects, but that's when the pressure really kicked in. I now had close to one hundred thousand people subscribed to my YouTube channel. That was almost as much as Orabrush had on their YouTube channel. I felt like I had been handed a golden ticket, something so many talented people work so hard to get, and I would feel so embarrassed if I let that go to waste. I did not want to be known as a one-hit wonder. I pulled out my phone and started writing down ideas for videos I thought I could do. I thought some of them were good, but none had the potential of the mistletoe video. When I had told people I would make more videos, I said it because I figured it wouldn't be that hard to come up with more entertaining ideas. But as I looked at my list, I realized I had a lot of work to do.

> JUST SO YOU KNOW, THE INTERNET IS A BIG PLACE. THERE'S ALWAYS ROOM FOR THE NEXT BIG YOUTUBER. THERE'S ROOM ENOUGH FOR EVERYONE.

14

THE START OF SOMETHING NEW

I thought I was going to continue struggling to come up with more great video ideas, but instead, the complete opposite happened. I couldn't *stop* coming up with viral ideas. Right off the bat, I started releasing videos every week and, every month, at least one of them would go viral.

My next big video happened in January, almost a month after the "Mistletoe Kissing Prank." Since the Orabrush was a product that helped prevent people's bad breath, it got me thinking about the social norm of bad breath. Would someone actually be honest enough to let me know I had halitosis? I talked to Kaitlin to see if she wanted to join me on this experiment and she was completely in support of the idea . . . until I told her we were going to have to abandon all oral hygiene for three days and eat nothing but junk food, onions, and garlic. It took a lot more convincing, but eventually she agreed to help with the video.

IS HONESTY REALLY THE BEST POLICY?

Recently, BYU had been named the most honest college in America, so it was the perfect setting to make our video. Our plan was to walk up to people and tell them we were on our way to a very important interview or date, and we just wanted to make sure our breath was okay. The day of the shoot, Kaitlin and I met up, had a very strange breakfast of items that would leave our breath smelling nasty, and walked onto campus. We wanted the reactions to be 100 percent genuine, so we had a friend with a camera record the interactions from far away. He gave me the signal he was ready, and I waited for an honest-looking person to walk by. The taste in my mouth was so bad it almost made me throw up. I would have much rather smelled a porta-potty than have to smell this all day. I was certain if anyone told me my breath was fine, they would be flat out lying. I saw a group of girls approaching, and I thought they would be the perfect people to ask.

"Hey, may I ask you a question?" I asked politely.

"Sure!" one of them responded.

"I'm on my way to a date and I know this is kind of strange, but can you smell my breath and tell me if it's okay?"

The looks on their faces were as if no one had ever asked them a question like that before . . . which didn't surprise me. It took them a while to say anything, and I started to wonder if maybe this idea wasn't going to work, or if maybe they knew it was some sort of prank.

Then one of the girls nervously piped up, "Yeah sure, I'll let you know."

I leaned in toward her face, put my mouth a few inches from her nose and blew the smelliest breath of air right at her. Because it was cold outside, I could see the condensation from my breath enter her nose, and I was certain she had inhaled the smell. I waited anxiously for a response. You know that look people make when they are trying to figure out the best way of telling you something without hurting your feelings? That was her face times ten. I knew she was wondering whether she should be honest with me.

"What do you think?" I asked. "You think I'm okay?"

CHAPTER 14

"Yeah, you're fine. It's not bad," she responded.

"Are you sure?" I clarified.

"Yeah, you should be good," she said.

Wow. I could not believe that just happened. Maybe my breath wouldn't make flowers wilt, but it was definitely not fine or good. Before they left, I told them I was actually doing a social experiment and pointed out the camera. They laughed out loud about having just been caught on camera and I then took this chance to ask for the girl's honest opinion.

"Okay, I'll be honest . . . it actually is pretty bad," she confessed.

I couldn't believe it. Even on one of the most honest college campuses it was still hard to be honest to someone about their bad breath.

Not everyone was so shy though. I reunited with Kaitlin and we traded approaching people and breathed out nasty garlic onion breath in their faces. Some people were completely honest with us, but lots of people were still too shy to tell us the truth.

I got back to the Orabrush office after a long day of filming, brushed my teeth, and started editing the video. I felt like I had another winner on my hands.

ANOTHER VIRAL VIDEO

"Bad Breath Prank" was a hit on YouTube. It got over a hundred thousand views in its first week. It was featured on several popular websites and Kaitlin and I even got asked to do a radio talk show interview. As I did the interview, I realized it was one of the same talk shows I would listen to while I was driving around cleaning porta-potties. I couldn't help but think about how far I had come in such a short time and how ready I was for more.

And more kept coming. The following month my next viral video happened when I released the "Spider-Man Kissing Prank." It had proved to be successful to lower a tiny mistletoe from a second story in front of people, so lowering a full-grown man dressed in a spidey-suit probably wouldn't be any different. It certainly was just as entertaining as mistletoe, but definitely a lot more difficult. If you watch the "Behind the Scenes" for the "Spider-Man Kissing Prank," you'll see why.

BECOMING MY OWN BOSS

It was now the middle of February in 2013 and my channel was having a ton of success. I had nearly two hundred thousand subscribers, just passing the total number of subscribers Orabrush had. I had just filmed the "Spider-Man Kissing Prank" and wanted to immediately get started on the edit, but my projects at Orabrush were taking all of my time. I had a crucial decision to make. Continue working at Orabrush and sacrifice the time I could give making my videos, or leave the job that had given me so much already and pursue my own interests and talents.

After battling over the decision for a few days, I decided I would leave Orabrush and work on building my own YouTube channel. My reasoning was that I figured Orabrush, or a job similar to it, would always be around; however, the chance to make my own stuff, wouldn't be. I needed to strike while the iron was hot, and right now, my YouTube channel was coming out of the forge.

On February 13, 2013, only six months after I started working there, I left my job at Orabrush for good. As sad as it was leaving my porta-potty job, it was even sadder leaving Orabrush. That job truly was an answer to my prayers. I asked them why they even hired me based on the little experience I had when I started. Their answer was that they just had a feeling it would be the right thing to do. I am forever grateful for the faith they had in following that feeling. That time was a stepping stone for me to get to where I am today.

The same day I left Orabrush, I uploaded the "Spider-Man Kissing Prank." Yep, you guessed it. It was a hit. This one didn't go "viral" like my other one's had. It didn't get picked up by news sites or blogs, but it steadily gained hundreds of thousands of views a week and is one of my most popular videos to this day.

DON'T BE AFRAID
TO TAKE A STEP
INTO THE UNKNOWN.
YOU MAY DISCOVER
OPPORTUNITIES YOU
USED TO ONLY DREAM
OF.

15

THE RISE

Now being completely on my own and being my own boss, I had to set my own rules and my own motivation. One goal I set was to have five hundred thousand subscribers on my channel by VidCon 2013. VidCon is an annual YouTube conference in Anaheim, California, where all of the biggest YouTubers in the world gather and meet with fans, do panels, and set up collaborations with other YouTubers. I figured if I had five hundred thousand subscribers by then, lots of people would want to work with me and I would also have more fans wanting to meet me.

To motivate me to accomplish this goal, I wrote on the whiteboard in my room, "You're only as good as your next video." I didn't want to get comfortable with the success I had with my previous videos and always wanted to have the mentality that my next video had to be my biggest. And it worked. A few weeks after my "Spider-Man Kissing Prank," I made a video just as big as the "Mistletoe Kissing Prank."

DO YOU BELIEVE IN MAGIC?

Around the same time my "Mistletoe Kissing Prank" went viral, a college friend of mine, who was into magic, left a deck of cards on my kitchen table. I picked them up and tried to remember any tricks I could from my elementary school days. I hadn't performed much since then. Nothing was coming to mind, so I downloaded a magic app and started learning a few tricks, but nothing worth showing to anyone outside of my apartment.

In March I got invited to a YouTube meetup called Playlist Live. It wasn't as big as VidCon, but there were still a lot of people there, and a lot of people I wanted to remember me. I realized I'd forgotten my business cards, so I went out and bought some playing cards to use instead. I knew it would be stupid and forgettable to just write my name on a Post-it Note for people. I had to do something memorable.

I couldn't just write my name on a random card and hand it over to everyone I met either. I had to make each encounter unique. So, I devised a simple plan. When I needed a business card to exchange information, I'd do a simple card trick and write my information on the chosen card to give away.

People *loved* it.

And it was kind of fun.

A few fans and even some popular YouTubers encouraged me to start doing magic tricks on my YouTube channel, but I just laughed at the idea. I mean, I didn't want my channel to become a "magic" channel. But the more I thought about it, the more I wondered if the rest of my fans would like card tricks too.

> LISTEN TO THE PEOPLE AROUND YOU. THEY MAY BE ABLE TO SEE THINGS IN A WAY YOU NEVER WOULD HAVE.

CHAPTER 15

THE MAGIC KISSING CARD TRICK

As I was doing the one trick I knew for people at Playlist Live, someone asked me if I knew the trick where two cards switched places in people's mouths. I told them I didn't but it sounded pretty cool, so I decided to learn it. I found a simple tutorial for it on YouTube and as I watched, I realized that this trick would be funny if it involved a kiss. The cards were already switching places, and what if I made it seem like it was because of the kiss? So far the kissing pranks had done really well for me, so it might be a safe way to introduce magic into my channel without losing any fans.

I shot the video, edited it, and nervously uploaded it to YouTube. I was fully ready with a good apology for my fans that hated the video, and even willing to delete the video if it got too many dislikes. The exact opposite happened. It immediately started getting shared on all the popular blogs. "Well, That's One Way to Steal a Smooch: Magician's Card Trick 'Requires' a Kiss from Participants in Order to Work" and "How Does He Do It? Magic Kissing Card Trick" were just a few of the titles. People were calling it "genius" and "the best magic trick ever." Just like the "Mistletoe Kissing Prank," this video got one million views in its first day. One of those views was by a man named Jimmy Fallon.

WHO'S THIS "JIMMY FALLON" GUY?

It wasn't uncommon for talk shows to feature my videos. Sometimes I even made a video call into their studio for an interview, but I hadn't yet had an actual television debut.

When the producers of *Late Night with Jimmy Fallon* emailed me about performing the trick on the show, I'll be honest, I didn't really know who Jimmy Fallon was. I'd heard his name before from this girl I knew. She mentioned how much she liked Jimmy Fallon, so when the show contacted me, I figured she might appreciate hearing about it from me first.

I went over to her house, talked with her for a few minutes, just being all cool and casual, then as I was leaving I said, "Oh, and I just got this email that I'm going to be on the Jimmy Fallon show."

She asked if I was serious, and when I confirmed that I really had been contacted by them, she freaked out. She was so excited that she kept hitting me with a pillow, which I'm still confused about to this day.

She made me sit down on the couch and watch his show segments that were posted on YouTube. I quickly realized how big of a deal he really was and wondered why in the world he would have me on his show.

I guess Jimmy Fallon was just browsing YouTube one day and saw my "Kissing Card Prank." He liked it. And when you have your own late night show and you like something you see on YouTube, you have the leverage to say, "Hey, come talk to me in front of millions of people and let's see what happens."

I didn't get overly excited, though. I'd already learned that talk shows don't always follow through. I was almost on Anderson Cooper's show when the mistletoe video went viral, but that segment was canceled the day I was supposed to fly out to New York.

I didn't want to be disappointed again, so I kept it pretty low key until I was actually on a flight to New York City. I brought my friend Nate (from the mistletoe video) along for moral support, and if for some reason they canceled, I'd have someone to hang out in New York with.

A CELEBRITY IN NYC

We arrived at NBC studios in Rockefeller Plaza and went inside to the studio for a dress rehearsal. I was feeling calm and collected up to this point, but for some reason, as we were standing under the lights and cameras walking through my part, I started to have second thoughts about coming out here.

The producers told me to walk through the trick saying word for word what I might say during the actual performance. I stumbled over my words and I even messed up the trick a little. I asked for more time to practice it, but they sent us back to our dressing room because they needed to get ready for the start of the show. As we walked back to our room, I passed by the dressing room of another one of the guests that would be on the show that night. Guess who it was . . . ANDERSON COOPER! I couldn't believe it. A few months ago I was going to be on his show, and now, I was so popular that we were guests on the same show together. That really boosted my confidence.

Back in the dressing room, Nate and I stuffed our faces with the free chips and cookies the show had provided for us. We even stuffed some in our bag so we could eat them later in the hotel. It was really great having Nate there because he helped keep my nerves down.

After nearly an hour of waiting, they called me to the stage and told me I was about to be on. That was when I saw the audience for the first time. When I did the rehearsal, the studio was empty, but now it was full of people. While yes, nine million people had seen my "Magic Kissing Card Trick," up to this point, that wasn't a live audience I was performing to. The last time I had performed magic for a group this size was back in elementary school and the trick didn't work. I was really hoping I wouldn't have a repeat like that. Jimmy finished up his interview and then said, "When we come back, we have YouTube sensation Stuart Edge in the studio to show us a magic trick."

Oh wow this is really happening. The producers put me in place to get ready for the performance. After a while, Jimmy came over and got into place too.

"Hey man, thanks for coming! You excited?" he said.

I didn't know what to say. I really wanted to chat, but I would much rather focus on making sure I got the trick right. I kind of just nodded my head and told him thanks for bringing me out here.

The producers called out that we were seconds away from being live again. Then the lights went on and Jimmy started his lines. "Hey everybody, we are back with the man behind the Stuart Edge YouTube channel which has blown up to almost forty-two million views with one viral video after another . . ."

I noticed Jimmy was reading from a cue card word for word which made me wonder if that's why they had me be so specific with my wording in the dress rehearsal. That would be such a relief if they had my words written down. I could read off the cards, and just focus on making sure the trick was done right.

Jimmy continued reading, "Please welcome in his first television performance, Stuart Edge, everybody!" The band played and the crowd cheered as I stood there waving with a deck of cards in my hand. Jimmy turned to me and said, "I watched this thing and I loved it. I think it was the first time I saw you, and then I went back and watched your other videos . . . do you know how to do magic tricks?"

I looked at the cue cards to read what my lines were, and all I saw on the card was RESPOND written in big black letters. *What?! They didn't write down my lines? Why did they have me recite my performance word for word then?* I opened my mouth and all I could say was, "Uh . . . apparently."

I realized that the cue cards were now gone and this performance was going to be whatever I wanted to make it. I was in the spotlight again and this was my show. I felt like little elementary school Stuart . . . cool and calm and ready to perform.

I answered Jimmy's question by giving quick explanations about my videos and how I came up with the idea for the "Magic Kissing Card Trick" and then went on with the performance.

The whole time I was performing, I was completely in my element. I remembered the reason I started making videos in the first place—because I loved the feeling of performing and I wanted to inspire people. I had Jimmy and the audience laughing just like I did in my show in elementary school, except this time really mattered.

When the performance was over, Jimmy ended giving me the best shout-out I've ever received, "Dude, I love it! It's so awesome. I appreciate that so much! Stuart Edge! You've got to check out YouTube.com/StuartEdge for great viral videos!"

The producer yelled cut, and I stood off to the side, adrenaline still pumping from the performance I just gave. Jimmy came up to me and said how much he loved my performance. I was thinking, *Duh, you flew me out here to be on your show . . . I sure hope you loved it!*

He invited me to sit with him on the couch during the last musical artist. We couldn't really speak to each other over the noise of the music, so all I could think to do was look over at Jimmy and do a little awkward smile and nod my head acknowledging that the band indeed sounded good. I'll be honest, it was kind of awkward.

When the show was over, we left the studio, and a few people that were in the audience stopped me to tell me great job. I felt like a real celebrity that day.

SUCCESS COMES AT A PRICE

Being on Jimmy Fallon was great, but it was kind of like my first viral video in a way. There was an increase in pressure from my fans. I'd made it onto one talk show. What was I going to do next? How was I going to top Jimmy Fallon? *When* would I top that experience? That's what you call a "double-edged sword." It's good in that I made it. It's bad in that I will face the pressure of that appearance for the rest of my career. People will always wonder when I'll make something good enough to be invited back, or good enough to make it on the next big talk show. I know this, though: I will never be able to repay Jimmy Fallon and his team enough for having me on his show. I realize how blessed and lucky I was to be given a chance to be on a show only a handful of people in my position will ever get to experience. While, yes, the experience added some pressure to my career, it also laid a foundation of confidence that I could fall back on during tough times. If I ever have my own late night show someday, I hope I can remember to have a special spot for the "little guys" out there.

16

THE FALL

I was having tons of success with my videos following the "Mistletoe Kissing Prank." I went from two hundred thousand to three hundred thousand subscribers in one week alone thanks to the mistletoe video, and was well on my way to reach my five hundred thousand goal by VidCon in August.

Since magic was such a huge hit on my channel, I tried my hand at it . . . or should I say *sleight of hand*, eh eh. "My Signed Card Through Glass" video amazed people. I asked girls to pick any card from a deck and write the first six digits of their phone number on it. After placing their signed card back in the deck, I made a deal with them that, if I could find their card, they had to give me the last four digits of their number. Most of them giggled and accepted the bet, but one girl claimed she had a boyfriend, so even though she'd like to see the trick, she wouldn't follow through with the deal. I proceeded with the trick anyway and threw the deck of cards at the giant window next to us. The cards fell to the ground as you'd expect them to, but stuck on the *inside* of the glass, was her signed card. "Can your boyfriend do that?" I asked. She must have realized the current guy she was dating *couldn't* do something as amazing as that, and wanted to be with someone that could or she made up having a boyfriend, because she took her card and gave me the rest of the number. I'd like to think it was the first reason, but it was most likely the second.

While a lot of my videos up to that point were slightly juvenile (getting a kiss, getting a number, or pulling a funny prank on someone), I was service-oriented at my core and started looking for ways to use my channel to give back. The first thing I tried was giving flowers to moms on Mother's Day. The video wasn't viral, but a lot of people still liked it. I also used magic to turn a one dollar bill into a hundred dollar bill for some homeless people in my area. Again, I was prepared to apologize to my fans if they hated the video, but this video went viral, gaining millions of views in its first few days.

KING OF YOUTUBE

By the time VidCon was approaching, my channel was hot. Every month I was in the top ten most-subscribed-to channels on YouTube, sometimes being in the top five. I saw people in the comments calling me the new "King of YouTube." Everything I touched turned to viral gold. It almost felt too easy. Think of any social norm, figure out a way to put it to the test, throw in a magic trick or a kiss from a stranger, and *boom*, you have a viral video.

> DON'T BE AFRAID TO SET GOALS THAT MAY SEEM LOFTY. IF YOU REACH FOR THEM AND FAIL, YOU WILL STILL BE A LOT CLOSER TO WHERE YOU WANT TO BE, ESPECIALLY HAD YOU NOT MOVED AT ALL.

August finally rolled around and it was time for VidCon. As successful as I felt, I had decided VidCon would be the place to prove whether I had really "made it." I hopped off the plane in Anaheim and my friend Preston who joined me for the trip ran up behind me. "Stuart! You just passed five hundred thousand subscribers!"

Things had been so crazy in the weeks leading up to VidCon, I had forgotten about my goal. A year ago to that day I had been cleaning porta-potties and I hadn't even made my first video yet. I'm constantly amazed at the power of goal setting.

That week VidCon was a huge success. I left feeling inspired, like I was finally ready to do what I had been wanting—to collaborate with other YouTubers.

COLLABORATION IS THE KEY TO GROWING A SUCCESSFUL CHANNEL

I got back to Utah and messaged Andrew Hales, a popular YouTuber who did social experiments on college campuses around the state. Since our audiences were so similar, I figured he would be the perfect person to do a collaboration with. It was the start of a new school year, and students were returning to school. It was the perfect time to make a video.

I'd had at least one viral video each month for ten months in a row, and I really didn't want to break that streak now, especially so soon after VidCon. I knew I needed to come up with a viral idea, and quick. I had seen a video skit go viral where a guy swept a girl off her feet. I was sure if we did that, but with real girls, we would get real reactions and it was bound to go viral. The video "Sweeping Girls Off Their Feet" was born and we decided it would go on Andrew's channel. As we made the video, it felt really simple and innocent. We simply walked up behind girls and picked them up, literally sweeping them off their feet. Most of the girls laughed about it and thanked us, saying we had made their days.

Our prank was simple, but it got laughs. In fact, everyone we showed it to seemed to enjoy it and told us it was bound to go big. I uploaded it to YouTube, expecting it to be my eleventh viral video. It definitely was, but not in the way I'd hoped.

HAVING SECOND THOUGHTS

The first day was great for both of us. We both gained a ton of new subscribers, nearly ten thousand each in the first day, and the video was already approaching a million views. I was back to riding the wave, I thought. Little did I know that the next morning we were going to crash hard. In fact, I wouldn't just say crash. We were pounded into the ground by that wave, faces dragging across the sand, getting bumped and bruised by the weight of the water pushing down on us.

Morning came and with it came a call from a reporter asking to interview me about the video. I was pretty used to that so I handled it as I would any other interview. I answered him honestly, even as his questions became harder and more pressing. Within the hour, his article about Andrew and me was online.

It wasn't good.

Not that it wasn't written well, it's just that the entire article had nothing but negative things to say about Andrew and me. I was so confused! Why would someone write something so bad about a video that was doing so well? Plus, I wasn't a bad person! I did my very best to make people smile every day and give to those in need.

He hadn't used anything I had told him correctly. Throughout the day I watched the views and read through the comments on the video. Most of them were positive, but there were a few negative comments here and there. I sprawled out on my floor that night, overcome with feelings of anxiety. Did I make a mistake in making this video? I broke out in a cold sweat and fell asleep right there in the middle of my bedroom floor. My phone buzzed in the morning and I shot up, still dazed and confused, wondering if everything that had happened the day before had been a dream. I looked at my phone to see a text from a close friend of mine, "Hey, Stuart, hope you are doing okay. People at school are getting really angry about your video. You should take it down if you can." I checked the comments of the videos and sure enough, the contention and hate hadn't been a dream after all. This was no longer just my problem, but was beginning to reach into the lives of friends and family. It was all completely real and overwhelming.

I thought the ugliness would stop with that one interviewer and the YouTube comments, but pretty soon more articles started coming in criticizing us for the way we treated the girls in the video. We started to see it everywhere. Blogs that before had excitedly shared my videos were now writing disappointed articles about me. Was I not doing a similar video to what you just posted a week ago? Why are you angry at me now? I realized then that the "media" is not your friend. Horrible comments popping up about being chauvinists, about how the video was disrespectful to the women we picked up on the street and how we needed to consider other people before pulling our pranks. I got tweets that day from people saying I should "kill myself" and people like me "shouldn't be alive."

REMEMBER, ONCE YOU PUT SOMETHING ONLINE IT'S REALLY HARD TO GET IT BACK. IT SPREADS AND YOU'VE GOT TO LIVE WITH THE CONSEQUENCES FOREVER.

As much as I wanted my problems to go away, I was hoping everything was okay for the people in our video too. I never wanted to create something that would bring stress to someone else.

LISTEN TO THE HATERS

There are always going to be trolls and people who just don't like your videos, but sometimes there is truth to what the "haters" are saying. I mean, I thought the video itself was funny, and nobody got angry when we filmed it, but what other good did it have going for it? It didn't promote anything worthy. It didn't inspire anyone to go out and do something good. It just *was*.

And then I had to ask myself a harder question. What happened to me?

What made me think videos like that were even okay to make? At what moment did my mentality about that change? It's different when you're surprising someone with singing or flowers, but physically picking someone up without their consent at all? It was more than just the "Sweeping Girls Off Their Feet" video; what made me think it was okay to parade around, placing people in any situations that pushed them past their comfort zones? Was everything I had been doing completely wrong?

I had to sit down and ask myself more hard questions, analyzing my motives and my objectives over the past ten months. It made me give serious thought to my future and how all these choices and everything I'd posted already would affect that. It wasn't pleasant.

That's when I realized that for a long time I'd been acting like someone who wasn't really me, and I had to become my real self again. I had been too worried about what other people thought of me. I began to understand the meaning of the oft-quoted saying, "Be who you are and say what you feel, because those who mind don't matter, and those who matter don't mind."

STARTING OVER

I picked myself up off the floor, my heart now heavier than it had ever been, and looked at my calendar of scheduled videos. I had a few more kissing prank ideas written on my whiteboard along with some videos similar to sweeping girls off their feet. My hand rose to the words on the board and I vigorously erased all my ideas. It was time to start over. I needed to be an example of good and stand for virtue in all things, regardless of the outcome.

> **CHANGING SOMEONE'S LIFE FOR THE BETTER IS WORTH MUCH MORE THAN INCREASING YOUR FAME.**

As I thought about who I really am and what impression I wanted to leave with both the people who would interact with me personally, as well as those who would view my videos, I had to decide immediately what I wanted people to gain from the videos I posted online. Because whether you believe it or not, the media, the things we watch, have an enormous impact on who we become and how we act.

A REAL INFLUENCER

Albert Einstein said, "Setting an example is not the main means of influencing another, it is the only means."

Whether I liked it, I was an example to all those who saw my videos. I could either influence their lives negatively or positively.

There's a reason YouTube celebrities are called influencers.

17

THE REAL CRAPPY JOB

The next week, I decided I would make a positive video to show the world who I really was. While this video wouldn't justify my previous actions, I hoped it would at least show people I had learned a lesson and was moving in a different direction. My idea was simple—tip pizza delivery drivers a hundred dollars with a little bit of magic. Even though I made it for personal reasons, the video was widely popular, garnering millions of views and attracting seventy thousand new subscribers to my channel. It is interesting that in the times of our lives when we feel like we are least deserving of praise, we often receive the most blessings, leaving us even more humbled. However, despite the fact that my latest video was positive and had gone viral, I was still bothered by decisions I had made in prior videos.

I promised myself to make sure every future video had a purpose, but I struggled with how to convey that message to the rest of the Internet. Some people demanded more card tricks. Others wanted more dating or kissing pranks. I didn't want to make the kissing pranks anymore and I only performed card tricks because my fans demanded them. Card tricks just weren't really my "thing," but they got views and people liked them.

It wasn't all bad. I felt the support of a lot of my fans and many of them were even making videos in which they gave flowers to their mothers or strangers on the street. They said I had inspired them—and that was great! I love when I inspire people to be kind and to give back.

But on the flip side, some people were posting videos about making out with strangers on the street and other things that weren't in line with my beliefs. I was bothered about the online image I'd created for myself. It was hard to think I could have inspired those types of videos.

STARTING FRESH

In January of 2014, I went through my entire channel and deleted anything I felt gave the wrong impression or anything that looked too immature to represent who I really was.

Even still, for the next six months, the pressure to make the videos other people wanted to see while trying to figure out who I was continued to grow. I was not enjoying it *at all*. I seriously wanted to quit making videos and go back to my old job cleaning porta-potties. At least my instructions in that job were clear, my route was defined, and I could clock out at the end of the day.

I could never clock out of being Stuart Edge.

After a lot of reflection, I realized the reason I was feeling this way was because I wasn't doing the things that were making *me* happy. I was making videos that made *other* people happy, and the videos *they* thought were fun . . . but I was forgetting about myself in the heart of it all. Making videos became my job. I was working for all those who watched my videos. They were what made me able to make a living on YouTube. If I ignored what they wanted, where would that leave me? Then again, if I simply worked for my fans, did that make my YouTube career any better than having a nine-to-five job?

CHAPTER 17

WAKE UP AND DANCE

The solution to my problems had already been taught to me by a nine-year-old boy named Andres. I had this idea for a video where I would dance behind people without them knowing. But I was afraid that if I did, people would unsubscribe from me because they thought it wasn't "funny enough" or it wasn't really a "prank."

After being so discouraged with the way my life was, I decided I was going to make the video anyway. I flew out to New York City with my friend RJ and started filming. The plan was for RJ to hide with the camera and film as I danced behind strangers. It was one of the hardest videos I'd ever filmed. Of the first two days we were there, I froze nearly every time I tried to dance because what I was doing was so uncomfortably awkward. Every time I found a person I wanted to dance behind, they would either leave before we could start filming or turn around too quickly and glare at me for standing so close. I've never felt more shut down in my life.

On our last day in New York, I woke up knowing that if I didn't force myself out of my comfort zone, we would leave without a video and the entire trip would be in vain. I went back onto the streets, and after a pep talk from RJ, failed miserably on my first attempt. I mentally reset and faked a smile, a tactic I used often as a young missionary. Again, the pressure of knowing that today was our last chance to film pushed me to put myself in uncomfortable situations and dance, regardless of how awkward I felt. After a few more hours of filming, and a lot of failed attempts, we headed back home without knowing if we had gotten enough shots to make a video.

I left New York feeling so relieved and accomplished at just having made the efforts though. As I started editing the video, a new wave of energy began streaming through me. I was excited about making videos again!

An added bonus was that people *loved* the video. I still get messages to this day from people letting me know how much that video inspired them. I'm glad, because it's one of my favorites as well.

To this day, anytime I am feeling in a rut, or need a boost of energy, I will make a dance video. If you are ever feeling down on your luck or just need a little pick me up, get up and dance!

18

I'M NOT DONE YET

The "Dancing with Strangers" video gave me that added boost of confidence I needed to get back to making the videos that I wanted to and that matched my personality. I started incorporating more of my talents into my videos: singing, playing the guitar, and even acting. I was able to feature people like Alex Boyé, Peter Hollens, Lindsey Stirling, Logan Guleff, and Shay Carl in my videos. I even had a few videos shared by Justin Bieber, Carly Rae Jepsen, and Chris Pratt.

As I look back on my post-dancing-with-strangers videos, I have loved every single one of them and am proud of the work. My channel started to turn into something that would sustain me even when I have a family someday. I don't think my future wife would have liked it if I woke up every day and was like, "Bye, honey! I'm off to film another kissing prank! This one's for *sure* going viral so we will be able to get that new bed for the baby!" As simple as it may seem, I no longer feel embarrassed when people recognize me, because I am confident with who I am.

WHAT IS SUCCESS?

Now I'd like to take a moment and talk about what I feel true success is. While I do feel that numbers are a big measure of success, particularly in the YouTube business, they can't be the only indicator of it.

If you define success solely using numbers, then you would take a look at my channel and say I was the biggest flop in YouTube history. In my first year and a half of making videos, 2,300,000 people subscribed to my YouTube channel. At the time of writing this book, another year and half later, only 150,000 more have subscribed.

> "TO BE YOURSELF IN A WORLD THAT IS CONSTANTLY TRYING TO MAKE YOU SOMETHING ELSE IS THE GREATEST ACCOMPLISHMENT."
> —RALPH WALDO EMERSON

A year and a half to get 2 million. Two years to get 150,000.

I'll admit, sometimes that's not easy for me to acknowledge. I know I am capable of having my numbers higher than ever before, but I don't want to do it at the expense of my integrity this time.

Now, some may argue that YouTube algorithms and all the technical stuff had a factor in it, and while I feel that could be true in some areas, I'd like to think there was a bit more divine intervention involved. The *moment* after I posted the "Dancing with Strangers" video, my number of subscribers stopped growing and my videos stopped going viral every week. One could argue that I have stopped posting creative videos—but I have worked harder since that day and have put out the content I am most in love with. Yet for some reason, my numerical success wasn't the same. People sometimes comment, "Your videos aren't as funny as they once were" and "Go back to the old stuff." I appreciate great feedback, and I have used those comments as motivation to keep pushing me to the next level, but why tell someone what they should be?

Everyone goes through stages of growth, followed by mistakes, followed by a change in direction and more growth. *Everyone* goes through it. What would life be without growth?

The difference is that most people go through these stages and change in their own private lives. Celebrities go through it publicly, and are often slammed and harassed by the media or their fans for the mistakes they make.

That has to be one of the hardest things about being so public—people think they know me, *really* know me, and then I'm judged based upon their perceptions. People may assume my life is simple, that it's full of happiness and success, but they don't know my struggles or my private thoughts any more than I know theirs. They don't see all the videos I turn down so I can stay true to my morals and beliefs. They don't know who I really am when I'm not in front of the camera, or who I'm becoming each day.

MAKE A DIFFERENCE TODAY.

I guess if I had to say who I am at my core, I am just a regular guy who wants to make a positive impact on the world.

Thomas S. Monson, president of The Church of Jesus Christ of Latter-day Saints said, "May we begin now, this very day, to express love to all of God's children, whether they be our family members, our friends, mere acquaintances, or total strangers. As we arise each morning, let us determine to respond with love and kindness to whatever might come our way."[1]

Since June 2014, when I filmed the "Dancing with Strangers" video in New York City, not much has changed in my life. I am still trying to figure out who I am. That's why I feel like I'm not done yet. In most fictional stories, after realizing what he to do, the hero saves the princess from the dragon's lair and then rides off into the sunset with her.

At this time in my life, I've figured out what I need to do, and I am engaged in a fiery battle with an ugly dragon. I won't quit until he is slayed and I have saved my princess. Unless of course I get that long-awaited phone call from the girl of my dreams—then I'll stop fighting because why save somebody else's princess?

NOTE

1. Thomas S. Monson, "Love—the Essence of the Gospel," *Ensign,* May 2014.

19

A NEW ENDING

I remember walking across the Golden Gate Bridge on my trip to California shortly after returning home from my mission. It was a beautiful sight to see, but what really impacted me was all the emergency phones along the bridge for people who were thinking about jumping.

That was sad, realizing that people would give up on life when there's so much more to live for. It reminded me of a quote that says, "You can't go back and make a new start, but you can start right now and make a brand new ending."[1]

Even I've made mistakes and gone into places that I shouldn't have, but I get to choose my own ending. I get to decide how my story will play out. We all get to make that choice.

WHAT LIES AHEAD?

We may not know what lies ahead of us for years to come, but we can move forward a few feet or maybe even a few inches, enduring the crappy moments with a smile on our face.

As we move forward, we find the path we need to take. For now, my path is online videos. I don't believe this is my last endeavor or the last interest I'll pursue, but I do believe it's preparing me for my next big thing.

After all, God has a plan for me and I'm excited to see what that is. I also believe that God is interested in those things that interest me. He wants me to be happy and he wants me to use my talents to spread good messages throughout the world. If there's a better way to do that than what I'm doing now, He'll help me find it. I feel like the day I can say I'm done is the day I die. But religiously, that's not accurate either, because I don't believe we quit existing at death. Which means I will continue to grow, progress, and learn long after I leave this life.

I'm pretty certain that when we die and we're standing before God, He's not going to say, "You have a million YouTube followers?! Here's your VIP ticket to heaven!"

It's not about numbers to Him. It's about our hearts.

Those "crappy moments" we go through in this life are put there to help us become better people. Our struggles are never in vain. My struggling through the night at Scout camp, all the way to the struggle I have had while writing this book, will all be for my good. The same is true in your life. During difficult times, I find solace in this scripture:

> And if thou shouldst be cast into the pit, or into the hands of murderers, and the sentence of death passed upon thee; if thou be cast into the deep; if the billowing surge conspire against thee; if fierce winds become thine enemy; if the heavens gather blackness, and all the elements combine to hedge up the way; and above all, if the very jaws of hell shall gape open the mouth wide after thee, know thou, my son, that all these things shall give thee experience, and shall be for thy good. (D&C 122:7)

THE END?

For those of you who wanted to read my story, this is about it—for now. I'd love to know how it impacted you, so as

CHAPTER 19

I mentioned at the beginning of the book, feel free to send me a message if something stuck out to you.

There are a lot of projects I am currently working on that will open many doors for me. I'm not exactly sure what's ahead. . . . I know I will always continue to do things that amaze and inspire. Maybe I'll host my own show or act in a movie. I might even try my hand at pursuing more of my musical abilities. Whatever I do, I know I will love it, and I know many of you will be there to support me along the way. For that, I will be forever grateful.

NOTE

1. James R. Sherman, *Rejection: How to Survive Rejection and Promote Acceptance* (Gilsum, New Hampshire: 1982).

YOUTUBE APPENDIX

I would love to give you a few YouTube pointers. Now, I must say, the best way to figure out how to be a successful YouTuber is to watch YouTube videos. While there are so many secrets for how to be successful online already available on the Internet—from which cameras to use, to which day and time might be best for posting a video—and so much that can be learned by asking others, you will grow a lot more if you search out the answers yourself.

That being said, here are some of my tips:

- Take time to plan out the videos you want to make. Sometimes we think the true talent is in how well someone can improvise a video on the spot, but taking time to plan out your video, even if it's just a vlog, will make it so much better.
- That being said, you never know what you're capable of until you try. You can sit for hours, wondering if a video will work or what new idea you should try. Sometimes the best thing to do is just start.
- You can make money from ad revenue on YouTube, but I would not make that your main reason for doing videos. I would look for other sources of income outside

of ad revenue. Try selling a product or merchandise. That will be more sustaining than ad sense.

- There is always a brand new social app or website coming out or a reason to start a brand new YouTube channel for every new idea you have. While it is important to try out new things and find new audiences, don't spread your audience too thin. I would suggest picking two or three apps, and sticking to those. Your engagement will be a lot higher. Also, try to keep everything you do on one YouTube channel. Utilize the playlist feature and organize your videos with that.

- Collaborate. Seriously. This is the best way to grow anything. Try reaching out to other people that have the same size of following as you, and then go up from there. You should be able to give to the other person the same as, if not more than, what they will give to you. If you do want to collaborate with a YouTuber who is bigger than you, you need to make it as easy as possible for them to say yes. Have everything planned out and ready so that all they have to do is show up.

- The last thing I want to say, which I mentioned in Chapter 16, is listen to your haters. Don't engage in video comment fights—that's never helpful. But rather, always listen. I believe there is always some truth behind everything said. So, if someone says they don't like your video or they thought it was boring, instead of just calling them a hater and blocking them, try to see it from their point of view. You might just learn something that you can do to make your videos better the next time around. If you've done that, and you still think they are crazy, then maybe they are and you should just move on from that. But never forget to first listen.

YOUTUBE APPENDIX

I know there are probably a million things I forgot to say or people I forgot to thank. If so, I apologize, but I will do my best do make it up to you. Thank you for taking the time to read my book. Now, go out there and make a difference. STUART EDGE, OUT!